FUNDAMENTALS

by
Ed Kenerson

Copyright © 2017

Fundamentals
by Ed Kenerson

Printed in the United States of America

ISBN 9781630500283

All rights reserved solely by the author. The author guarantees all contents are original and do not infringe upon the legal rights of any other person or work. No part of this book may be reproduced in any form without the permission of the author. The views expressed in this book are not necessarily those of the publisher.

Scripture quotations taken from the Holy Bible, New International Version (NIV). Copyright © 1978 by Moody Press. Used by permission. All rights reserved.

www.FreeChristianPublishing.com

Table of Contents

The Foundation: Devoted Dedication
A Step of Faith...page 7

Awesome Evidence...page 12

Good News...page 18

Our Core Conviction...page 24

The Framework: Disciplined Discernment
Building Tip#1: Always Be Watching...page 30

Building Tip#2: Always Be Wanting...page 35

Building Tip#3: Always Be Willing...page 40

The Furnishings: Demonstrated Discipleship
Integrate Your Life...page 46

Always Stay Pure...page 51

Let Others Into Your Life...page 57

Master Your Fears...page 62

Jesus...On Prayer...page 67

Breaking Bad Habits...page 71

Avoiding Compromise...page 75

Golf and Grace...page 80

Is Your Worship Genuine?...page 85

Failure Happens...page 90

Demons and Demigods...page 94

Facing Your Goliaths...page 100

Know Yourself...page 105
The Expectation of Blessing...page 109
There's A Price To Be Paid...page 113
Male and Female...page 117
Who's Holding Your Ladder...page 126
"But...It Feels So Good"...page 129
Who's Driving...page 133
Abigail's Wisdom...page 138
Pain and Gain...page 143
"Not Again!" ...page 148
Short or Long Distance Running...page 154
Your "Wish List" ...page 158
Living In A PC World...page 162
Fantasy Verses Reality...page 166
Living In A Battle Zone...page 172
The Honest Truth...page 177
The "Two" of Me...page 181
Theocracy, Theology and Practicality...page 185
Biting The Bait...page 191
How Deep Is Your Well...page 195
Learning To Love...199
Servanthood and Ministry...204
Giving It Your All! ...page 208

Introduction

As a young boy of ten, I had the privilege of watching our house being built in the then rural town of Cheshire, Connecticut. My parents bought 6 acres of land, which had an old rustic cabin sitting on a small knoll half way up a wooded hill. We got there in late spring and started building our new home around the cabin, which would ultimately become the living room in the middle of this 75' long, split level ranch. I remembered all the fun and learning experiences I had growing up there in my book, "The Cabin In The Woods."

This book applies the construction process to building a strong and enduring spiritual house for believers. There are 3 overall areas of spiritual application, with short, topical teachings within each area. At the end of each topic is what I refer to as **Your Spiritual Tool Box**, a strategic guide for spiritual construction.

You'll also see the **Today's Project** and the **Your Blueprint** categories, which probably need no explanation. But, the **Keeping It Plumb** topic is something you may not be familiar with. A "plumb bob" is a tool dating all the way back to ancient Egypt for measuring vertical alignment. It's nothing more than a hanging string with a pointed weight at the end. I remember my uncle using it when aligning the walls of the new house. In our Christian walk, we need discernment, and this tool presents some thoughts on adjusting our lives in such a way as to keep things straight and in line with God's Word. I hope this spiritual tool box will be of great help to you as you build your own spiritual home in accordance with the *fundamentals* of God's Will.

Your Foundation:

Faith Commitment

The Christian life rests upon Jesus Christ and his death and resurrection. It's our primary spiritual conviction and life commitment. The problem, however, is that the world around us and our inner natures exist in antagonism to this fundamental truth. Inside, we constantly fight against doubt, anger, pride, lust and other rebellious enemies, all of which we wish would just go away at times. But, until we enter heaven or Jesus returns, these foes, along with Satan's demonic forces, forever wage war against our spiritual growth. This is why we must cling to our faith commitment, refusing to let go and always gripping it tightly as our fundamental purpose for living! This is the **foundation** for building a strong Christian walk.

A Step Of Faith

"The map says it's a step of faith, Indy," said his companion with a challenging smile.

The scene is from an Indiana Jones movie, when Indy is looking outwardly from inside a cave and down a mountainside crevasse. Stepping out from where he was would be certain death, for in front of him was a 1000' drop with no walk-way and a 25' jump to the entrance of a cave on the other side of the crevasse. Nevertheless, the path to the holy grail meant crossing it somehow.

"How can we cross?" someone exclaims. "It's impossible...I don't see anything to get us across."

"The answer on the map says that it requires a "step of faith," another responds. Indy pauses, then reaches out with one leg for a brief moment. He then commits himself, putting his full weight upon what he *believes* is there, but can't see...a step of faith. Instead of falling into the crevasse, however, he appears to be standing in thin air. Everyone is shocked, until someone picks up a handful of sand nearby and throws it out in front of Indy. The sand spreads out like tiny marbles upon an invisible glass walkway bridging the mountainside crevasse. Now, all are relieved and follow Indy across, walking carefully yet safely to the other side, where they resume their search for the illusive holy grail.

In the movie above, Indiana Jones can't really see the glass walk-way until it is evidenced by the sand. Even then, he still can't see it fully, but he assumes it is there, because of the sand. His places his faith in the map and in its instructions, takes a step and finds the confidence he previously didn't have. Seeing the sand wasn't a foolproof idea either, for there was no assurance that the bridge further on would hold anything more than sand. So, in this example, Indy reasoned and made several risky assumptions. His "sight" was really no more than intellectual conviction, upon which he trusted and risked his life.

There is probably no greater *untruth* passed around today than the statement "*seeing is believing.*" Why? Because buried within this expression is a *false* assumption about life, that we can know something absolutely, when we cannot. Only God sees and knows everything. We, however, "see in part," as the Apostle Paul reminded the Corinthians (II Cor. 5:7). Because we are not omniscient, everything we intellectually "see" (understand) is built upon a foundation of faith.

An atheistic scientist, for instance, may think Christians are foolish for believing things without proof. Yet, he or she trusts in scientific presuppositions, in experimental conditions and in the data or results gathered from a given project or experiment. That's not to say that all of his conclusions are wrong, but it is equally important to remember that not all such conclusions are of necessity true.

For all of us, **truth is trust**, for fact always involves faith at some level. I trust that my car will not fall apart at 65 mph on the highway. I trust that the chair I sit upon in my office will once again hold me up and not let me fall to the floor in disapproval. I enjoy the phrase that so often accompanies medical advertising on the television: "Only your Doctor knows for sure, so check with him or her first before trying ..." We trust that what the Doctor gives us will not hurt us, rather help us, but even this has no certainty.

Years ago, I learned a lesson about trust when accepting the counsel of a doctor (doctors by enlarge are committed, capable professionals, of course). However, at my graduation from seminary, I wrongly trusted in a resident doctor at the local hospital outside Boston, Massachusetts. Here's what happened.

While in line with 200 other graduating seniors waiting to enter the auditorium to get our diploma, I accidentally scratched my eye with the 3x5 card given to us to hand to the Dean before walking across the stage. It hurt a bit, but the watering eye was more embarrassing to me than anything else. Though I made it through the whole ceremony fairly well, upon arriving at my apartment with my wife and parents to celebrate, I had to lie down and just rest. My eye was now hurting quite a bit. Finally, after my parents and guests left, I went to the emergency room to get some medicine for the pain. The doctor "on call" looked at it and prescribed some eye drops to take every four hours. I returned and faithfully applied them through the night. Unfortunately, I suffered through the whole night, for the scratch increased in pain and watering. Eventually, we called a good friend, whose father was a prominent eye specialist in the Boston area. He agreed to see me that Sunday morning at his office, and was I glad I did so. The medicine the original doctor prescribed was incorrect and opened up the cornea scratch even more. After getting the right medicine and applying it over the next few days, my eye quickly healed.

My point is that life across the board involves trust and faith at *every* level and in *every* circumstance, though we may not always recognize it...and that's okay. This is also true when talking about evidence for the existence of God.

To say that God doesn't exist, for instance, flies in the face of the *evidence*. Physical, moral, social and scientific truth *does* exist (suggesting that we're more than purposeless, design-less and amoral life forms). Like it or not, absolute truth, along with reliable, repeatable and resilient life principles, exists all around us. We are not perfect in our understanding of it all, for sure, but to deny absolute truth is to deny the trustworthiness of proven principles of science, mathematical equations, logic, physical laws, and the existence of both knowledge and wisdom. To refute all this (if one is foolish enough to do so) only plunges one into a world of physical illusion and purposeless moral bankruptcy. But, that's where some atheists, agnostics and moral libertarians want us to go, today, right?

As believers, however, we understand that truth exists *because* God exists; there is no other logical and obvious way to have it. Christian or non-Christian, we must accept that absolute truth exists, or we have no sensible and secure way of living. It is logically absurd to deny it, morally blind to avoid it, and practically dangerous to live against it. And, along with this is the underlying reality that faith is woven into the fabric of everything we know about truth and life.

Therefore, when it comes to building our *spiritual house*, trust is also an important part of the process. Even though we cannot escape our own limited intellectual insights, *this shouldn't discourage us,* for God created us this way and knows our limitations. *God doesn't demand absolute certainty on our part (which isn't possible, anyway).* We just need to *trust* in the living and written Word of God.

Now, trust in general can be passive and unintentional, like so many common things we do in the course of our day...riding in the car, walking down the steps, using a credit card to pay for something, etc. On the other hand, trust can also be a very *intentional* thing, where we choose to face the continuous difficulties and unrelenting pressures of life with a *fundamental* belief in God's purposeful will. Of course, faith alone is not the complete answer for every need or issue, but it certainly is the foundational part of the structure necessary for building a well-constructed spiritual house. And, that's what we're talking about in this book.

Now, let's dig a bit deeper. "How about *you*? Do *you* believe in Christ as your Savior and Lord?" You probably would say, "Yes...yes, of course, I do, Ed."

Great. So, here's a more precise question: "How *deeply* do you and I believe and trust in Christ as your Savior and Lord?" Humm...

Traveling down the highway of spiritual trust and faith is how we first found forgiveness for sin and eternal life in Jesus Christ. It was a directional choice we made at a single point in time. Okay...understood. But, *how consistent* have you and I been while travelling down that road thereafter? Are we *staying* in that believing and trusting relationship as we go about our lives? Or, do we too often get *side-tracked* by detours of doubt and side-swiped by seasons of sin.

"Faith may seek to "see" all that it can, but it needs only to believe what it must. It searches for certainty, but it rests in God's sovereignty."

The key to all this is to understand that faith in Christ is more than just an initial step, something that we've *left behind* and to which we never return. Rather, it is similar to the frame on your automobile that holds everything together... tires, steering, engine, fuel, seats, shocks, transmission. Automotive manufacturers don't tie a steering wheel to the gas tank or weld seats to the engine. No, everything has a proper place, but it is all held together directly or indirectly by the vehicle frame (for heavier, commercial vehicles) or a unibody structure (most cars).

Similarly, *Gospel faith is that which holds everything together safely in our relationship with God.* Believing trust in Christ must continually energize us, if we allow it to, when facing spiritual hills, hazards and highway mishaps. It helps us persevere through difficulties, stress and demonic attacks that would otherwise bring disaster. Too many believers get unnecessarily

"Faith is not just a point in time, but a process in progress."

lost or unfortunately detoured from consistency simply because they fail to *stay secured* to this important spiritual mindset. Faith is not just a *point in time*, friends, but a *process in progress*.

The Apostle Paul gives us another illustration...we should "fight the fight of faith." He is emphasizing the *ongoing* nature of faith, particularly when encountering daily temptations and Satanic attacks. The prayers we speak and the inspiring verses we read in the morning will probably be quite dissipated by the end of the day, correct? So, of necessity, faith is the foundational resource we call upon to refresh our personal commitment and spiritual walk. It's a raw trust in Christ, enabling the believer to challenge doubt, to deny lust, to overcome fear, to reject temptation, to love the unlovely and to do whatever God commands.

Imagine if Daniel looked at the drooling, blood-thirsty lions in that Babylonian pit and exclaimed, "Well, I **guess** I trust in God's sovereignty and power?" Such is not very convincing to anyone...certainly not to the lions! In the same way, our belief in Jesus is something we must continually call upon to reassure and strengthen us in the face of difficulty. Fundamental faith moves us inwardly and outwardly to obey God. This is what Paul had in mind in Gal. 2:20:

> "I have been crucified with Christ and I no longer live, but Christ lives in me. The life I now live in the body, I live by faith in the Son of God, who loved me and gave himself for me."

Obedient faith...yes, that's the critical attitude capable of sending Satan running and which is consistently able to overcome our lingering lusts and pompous pride. Please remember, legitimate and obedient faith in Christ is that which **chooses** to follow Christ every moment of every day. If such a faith cannot be found at all in the life of someone claiming to be a believer, I am confident that it is illegitimate and characteristic of "professors," not genuine possessors.

Your Spiritual Tool Box

Today's Project:
Trust

Your Blueprint:
"For to me, to live is Christ and to die is gain." (Phil. 1:21)

Keeping It Plumb:
- Genuine faith in Jesus is more than intellectual, it's an ongoing attitude of obedient trust in the living God who saves us from hell.
- When answering the unanswerable and "unscrewing the inscrutable," be cognizant of your limitations. Know when to stop and trust. We don't live by explanations, but by faith.
- If besieged by doubt, exercise patience, and stay in obedience to the God's Word. God will give you what is necessary endure.

The Evidence Is Awesome!

In the last chapter, I discussed the *legitimacy* of faith. Like it or not, we see all things through the eye-glass of "propositional truth." That's a fancy name for saying that our assertions of what is true or not true are always based upon our finite nature. But, that's not to say that such faith is simply blind, or that we have no way of discerning truth from fiction.

Again, in this world of uncertainty, people must choose what to believe **by evidence and logic.** If something appears to be true, based upon what we understand the evidence to say, then we accept it. If not, we reject it and assume it to be false. Yes, any one of us can be wrong at times, but that doesn't mean we can't know truth and live by it. For instance, we don't question whether we can jump off a 10-story building for fun and live, or that we must eat in order to live or that sitting down and do nothing will make us rich. Of course not! **Life teaches us the truth** through experience and sound thinking.

As believers, we have chosen to believe and trust in Jesus Christ as our Savior and Lord...this is the foundation of our spiritual house. We don't do that "blindly," that is, without any evidence or logic. In this regard, let me suggest three *fundamental* types of evidence that support our belief in Christ.

- The Credibility of the Biblical Revelation
- The Credibility of the Gospel Message

- The Credibility of Personal Experience

God has revealed himself in his Son, Jesus Christ, and in the Bible

Have you ever heard of the destruction of Pompeii? It's an amazing historical event, which is estimated to have cost the lives of over 11,000 people. Pompeii was a vacation destination for many Romans and was situated in a beautiful and  agricultural location. It was *also* known for *extreme sexual immorality*.

"The eruption occurred on 24 August AD 79, just one day after Vulcanalia, the festival of the Roman god of fire. A multidisciplinary...study of the eruption...indicates that...heat was the main cause of death of people, previously believed to have died by ash suffocation. The results of the study, published in 2010, show that exposure to at least 250 °C (482 °F) hot surges (known as pyroclastic flows) at a distance of 10 kilometres (6 miles) from the vent was sufficient to cause instant death, even if people were sheltered within buildings. The people and buildings of Pompeii were covered in up to twelve different layers of tephra, in total 25 meters deep, which rained down for about six hours." (https://en.wikipedia.org/wiki/Pompeii)

If I said to you that the destruction of Pompeii was a clever hoax, you would think that I was crazy. You would then give me all the factual information you could gather to back-up your belief and to convince me of my historical error.

The truth is, Jesus Christ lived and walked this planet...*it's an historical fact, not a myth, and it's worthy of our trust.* He is not a cleverly devised story that was handed down and added to throughout history, though some liberal skeptics have tried to create such a scenario...and failed. Here's some facts about the historicity of his life from *just one* of many reliable sources from antiquity:

"Now there was about this time Jesus, a wise man, if it be lawful to call him a man, for he was a doer of wonderful works, a teacher of such men as receive the truth with pleasure. He drew over to him both many of the Jews, and many of the Gentiles. He was the Christ, and when Pilate, at the suggestion of the principle men among us, had condemned him to the cross, those that loved him at the first did not forsake him; for he appeared to them alive again the third day; as the divine prophets had

foretold these and ten thousand other wonderful things concerning him. And, the tribe of Christians so name from him are not extinct at this day." (Josephus in his "Antiquities, XVIII." 33)   Taken from Evidence "That Demands A Verdict," Here's Life Publishers, P.O. Box 1576, San Bernardino, CA,1991, p. 82

There are others, as well, that clearly testify to the *historical* existence of Jesus, and you can find those easily enough, if you desire. Christians can confidently assert that Jesus lived and taught the things he did, and this is without question, even to atheists and skeptics who disagree with his teaching. Again, one may not believe in what he taught, but he or she cannot historically refute his life, teaching and impact upon the world.

We should also remind ourselves that the Biblical Gospels (Matthew, Mark, Luke, John) were not written as a text for a new religion, as Mein Kampf was for the establishment of a new world order called Nazism. The Gospels were the simple, factual accounts of eyewitness writers who simply wanted to share the story and glory of Jesus' amazing life. The Gospels are the unpolished records of Jesus' miraculous manifestations and his profound teaching, which has literally changed the known world. Jesus' miracles and his resurrection exist within the pages of the Bible and this historical record stands firm and believable, despite the fruitless efforts of skeptics to disprove it since Jesus walked the face of this earth.

In addition to the historicity of Jesus' existence, the *Bible* also clearly affirms his claim to be the Son of God and, therefore, to be God incarnated.

> *"In the past God spoke to our ancestors through the prophets at many times and in various ways, but in these last days he has spoken to us by his Son, whom he appointed heir of all things, and through whom also he made the universe. The Son is the radiance of God's glory and the exact representation of his being, sustaining all things by his powerful word. After he had provided purification for sins, he sat down at the right hand of the Majesty in heaven."* (Hebrews 1:1-3)

> *"The Son is the image of the invisible God, the firstborn over all creation. For in him all things were created: things in heaven and on earth, visible and invisible, whether thrones or powers or rulers or authorities; all things have been created through him and for him. He is before all things, and in him all things hold together. And he is the head of the body, the church; he is the beginning and the firstborn from among the dead, so that in everything he might have the supremacy. For God was pleased to have*

all his fullness dwell in him, and through him to reconcile to himself all things, whether things on earth or things in heaven, by making peace through his blood, shed on the cross." (Colossians 1:15-20)

"I and the Father are one." Again, his Jewish opponents picked up stones to stone him." (John 10:30-31)

In addition, there is the "small" fact of the historicity of the resurrection of Jesus Christ. It has been attacked by "higher critics" but always without success. First, the Bible is solid in its assertion that Jesus rose from the dead. But, we've already shown that the Biblical record is convincingly strong and secure. Secondly, if Christ did not rise from the dead, the Bible by default *would* be a lie. Thirdly, if Christ didn't rise from the dead, the whole Christian message of sin and judgment is out the door. It would mean that the Gospel is false, that sin is not sin, that there is no such thing as evil and there are no moral absolutes. This also implies that divine judgment is not necessary, for mankind can live any which way it chooses. It would also mean that God has not credibly spoken to mankind, for there is no religion but Christianity that says that God has come to earth and spoken to mankind directly (though there are people who teach what they *believe* to be true about gods and spiritual realities...Buddha, Confucius, Mohammed, etc.).

"But if still His call we refuse
And all his wondrous love abuse;
Soon must He sadly from us turn,
Our bitter prayer for pardon spurn.
Too late, too late, will be the cry,
When Jesus of Nazareth
has passed by."
(Herb Lockyer)

"All religions talk about man reaching up to god, but in Jesus, God reached down to mankind."

There's another outstanding proof of the Bible's claim to be the actual word of God...it's *prophetic foundation*. Over 300 prophecies were made some 400 years before Jesus was even born and each one has been historically verified. Let me give you just a few:

- The place of his birth
- The form of his death (crucifixion)
- He would be born of a virgin
- His specific Jewish lineage

- He would be called Messiah and God
- He would bring healing
- He would die as a sacrifice for sin
- Soldiers would mock and gamble for his clothes
- He would be given vinegar to drink
- He would rise from the dead
- He would ascend to heaven

Some have tried to destroy the trustworthiness of the Bible in order to deny Jesus' claims regarding his divine person and purpose. However, the above record of prophetic fulfillment affirms that the Bible is God's Word. If a mechanic advertises that he can fix the broken transmission in your car, and he does so, then he has proven his claim. If the prophets of the Old Testament claimed *400+ years before Jesus was even born* that Messiah would be recognized by fulfilling what they said about him - and Jesus clearly did as out-lined above and beyond – then this alone justifies one's faith in him as Son of God and Savior of the world.

However, beyond all this, we can also trust the authority of the Bible, because of its incomparable *historical uniqueness*.

> *The closest work of antiquity is Homer's Iliad, written in 900BC. Of this, there are 643 copies, the earliest dating at 400 BC or 500 years from the original. The Bible, however, has nothing less than astounding historical trustworthiness regarding textual veracity. There are over 24,000 copies of the New Testament, the earliest copy being only 25 years from the original. Noted Scholar F.F. Bruce says, "There is no body of ancient literature in the world which enjoys such a wealth of good textual attestation as the New Testament."* (Taken from Evidence "That Demands A Verdict," Here's Life Publishers, P.O. Box 1576, San Bernardino, CA,1991, p. 42-43)

I believe we have over-viewed the trustworthy and *historical* foundation upon which rests the Christian Gospel. Countless pages of additional and supportive materials are available, which support the Bible and its historical integrity. Feel free, of course, to search out that information, if you desire to do so, for my presentation here is not a complete, in-depth apologetic for the Christian faith. My purpose in this is only to briefly acknowledge the already proven trustworthiness of the Christian record so that we as believers can have confident assurance that what we believe is true.

Your Spiritual Tool Box

Today's Project:
Rely On The Evidence

Your Blueprint:

*"For we did not follow cleverly devised stories when we told you about the coming of our Lord Jesus Christ in power, but we were **eyewitnesses** of his majesty. He received honor and glory from God the Father when the voice came to him from the Majestic Glory, saying, "This is my Son, whom I love; with him I am well pleased. We ourselves **heard** this voice that came from heaven when we were **with him** on the sacred mountain. We also have the **prophetic** message as something **completely reliable,** and you will do well to pay attention to it, as to a light shining in a dark place, until the day dawns and the morning star rises in your hearts."* (II Peter 1:16-19)

Keeping It Plumb:

Faith is never antagonistic to logical, physical and spiritual evidence. It builds upon these. So, enjoy the wealth of historical, scientific, psychological and experiential support with which God has blessed us to support our faith in Jesus Christ as Savior and Lord. There are so many good writers and books dealing with all this to call upon, we can readily share our faith with confidence. In this way, we can always, *"**be prepared** to give an answer to everyone who asks you to give **the reason** for the hope that you have."* (I Peter 3:15)

Good News

The Gospel is Sensible, Trustworthy and Proven

It's good to review our faith from a logical, philosophical and historical point of view, as we have just done in chapters one and two. However, our faith should not rest in our knowledge about such things alone. It is our *fundamental* knowledge of the "good news" – the Gospel of Jesus Christ – which should hold our deepest conviction.

Convictions are what we call life changing beliefs, and we'll be focusing upon these in upcoming chapters. However, the spiritual conviction we took hold of at the point of salvation is Gospel faith, which is foundational and moves us securely along in the process of our spiritual growth. So, what are the basic truths of this Gospel?

God Created Mankind For Relationship

Think with me for a moment about the doctrine of the Trinity…that God exists in three persons, Father, Son and Holy Spirit. This says something about God that is very important to our understanding of who he is. He is relational at the core of his being. From this, we understand that he seeks relationship with those whom he has created…you and I. This means that he wants ongoing communication with us; he wants harmonious love to be the environment of that relationship; and he desires unity and common purpose(s) to draw us together.

> *"Jesus replied, "This is the most important (commandment): 'Hear O Israel, the Lord our God is One Lord, and you shall love the Lord your God with all your heart and with all your soul and with all your mind and with all your strength."* (Mark 12:29-30)

> *"...In Him (Christ) and through faith in Him we may enter God's presence with boldness and confidence..."* (Ephesians 3:10-12)

> *"Come to Me, all you who are weary and burdened, and I will give you rest. Take My yoke upon you and learn from Me; for I am gentle and humble in heart, and you will find rest for your souls."* (Matt. 11:29)

People seem to fill up their lives with every pleasure and purpose *other* than God. If they do acknowledge him, they often compartmentalize him, assigning him a few hours a week for some "religious" type of setting. To say, however, that they have a relationship with God would be reaching too far. Their belief system and life experience allow no significant place for him to dwell or rule.

This probably paved the way for social commentators to report that "God Is Dead" in the rebellious 70's and 80's in America. By the way, that original statement was made by the German philosopher, Friedrich Nietzsche, in 1882. But, here's a quote that has truth to it:

> *"...all that now remains (in man) is the empty print and trace? This he tries in vain to fill with everything around him, seeking in things that are not there the help he cannot find in those that are...this infinite abyss can be filled only with an infinite and immutable object; in other words, by God himself."* (Blaise Pascal)

What Pascal is referring to is obvious to anyone who is honestly looking for reality...it's found in knowing God. The purpose of life is found in God and his will, not in self-satisfying things such as personal pleasures or great accomplishments. Without God everything falls apart, personally, socially and morally.

"Who am I? What am I living for? What's the meaning of life?"

When asking this, in my opinion, we indirectly acknowledge our need of an intimate relationship with God...or the question couldn't be asked. A meaningless, evolutionary and random existence based solely upon chance molecular interactions becomes emotionally and logically absurd. Realistic thinkers recognize a predisposed order in life, for godless existence would be nothing more than uncontrollable chaos. This is not what one sees when looking at the world around us.

So, the Gospel (or "good news") of Jesus Christ begins with God...his joy in creating us and his pleasure in seeking relationship with us. As believers, we accept this fundamental purpose of life not just because of its innate sensibility, but because Jesus came in human form to communicate it. He came in order that we might "see and touch" the message, not just hear it. Wrapped in miraculous garb and prophetic reliability, the message of Christ rings true to those willing to listen.

Sin Has Broken Our Relationship With God

Someone created the blueprint for the twin towers that unfortunately came down on the 9/11 tragedy. The blue prints were sound, except for the unforeseen dilemma that when each floor fell to the floor below it, the total collapsing weight exceeded the ability of the floors beneath to hold the load.

In the same way, God has created certain things in the spiritual world to be utilized according to his blue print. If we do our *own* thing, however, and exceed its spiritual specifications in opposition to his blueprint, we will experience evil consequences. Let me suggest how this is evidenced in life.

Imagine that I just made it into the hospital delivery room, late due to traffic from work, but excited. Suddenly, the nurse comes out and announces that my wife just delivered a healthy new born girl! The 8.5 lb. baby is doing great, and I can see her in about 15 minutes or so.

I turn to one of the other fathers who was also there in the room. "Wow," I say, "I was so nervous. But, everything went great...and I've got a perfect little girl!"

Quickly, the guy to my left becomes upset by my words. I notice that his clothing is tattered, shoes muddy and his demeaner very discouraged.

"Oh...yeah...that's good, I guess. I...a...just got the news that my wife (he starts to tear up) well, she didn't make it." He looks down at the floor, searching for an answer to his grief. "I ran over from work and got here as soon as I could, too, but...I just didn't get to say goodbye." (he begins sobbing)

Just then, the *guy* across the room, dressed in a suede sport coat, suddenly gets up as another well-dressed *guy* enters the room. They embrace.

"This is my wife. A friend of ours was artificially impregnated and the delivery was a success. We're excited that we can finally get to be parents. Everything worked out fine!" I stand there in disbelief regarding the cultural change that has infiltrated and infected our society. Still, none of us there wanted to be judgmental about such sexual perversion, so everyone offered plastic smiles.

Then, the guy to my right interrupts. "You know, not everyone is as lucky as you folks (he swears)!" *My* kid is in the ICU with some sort of complications. According to the nurse, he's going to have permanent brain dis-function (he looks angrily at me). I don't want to hear about your "perfect" child right now, okay!"

I'm now feeling bad that I said anything at all. Finally, I look around at the fourth father, who knows he's next in line to say something. "Well, I'm doing all right, I guess. The delivery went well and everything. But, I just don't know what to do about it all," he offers.

"What do you mean, friend...is your wife okay?" I ask.

"Yeah...but, that's my problem. She's not my wife, she's my girlfriend! How am I going to explain *that* to my wife, who thinks I'm just working late tonight? I just can't leave her, but I can't just walk away from my wife either. I think I'm just going to go out and get drunk!"

The above scenario isn't so strange or unrealistic, probably happening more often than we want to think. So, what happened to my perfect world? It seems that it's been invaded by things like death, disease, and deteriorating moral values. Whatever is good, is still there, of course. People of purpose and design still breath and live, healthy babies are still being born and moral choice is still talked about and sometimes practiced.

But, there is something else here, too, something that is corrupting and antagonistic to good...another force causing grief, loss, anger, jealousy, death and moral confusion. Does such a corrupting presence mean that God doesn't exist, that right and wrong don't matter, that we're all just unexplainable accidents in the cycle of haphazard evolutionary explosions without meaning and purpose?

Some would go down that moral road today, but to no avail. For, logic suggests that if evil does exist, then good must exist also, or one couldn't define evil as standing in opposition to it. Indirectly and subtly, therefore, evil actually reveals the existence of God, the author of moral truth and goodness.

> *"This is the message we have heard from him and declare to you: God is light; in him there is no darkness at all. If we claim to have fellowship with him and yet walk in the darkness, we lie and do not live out the truth. But if we walk in the light, as he is in the light, we have fellowship with one another, and the blood of Jesus, his Son, purifies us from all sin. If we claim to be without sin, we deceive ourselves and the truth is not in us. If*

we confess our sins, he is faithful and just and will forgive us our sins and purify us from all unrighteousness. If we claim we have not sinned, we make him out to be a liar and his word is not in us." (I John 1:5-10)

The word for sin in the original language of the Bible simply means "missing the mark." Sin is a category of thoughts, attitudes and behaviors that have missed the perfect *design* of God's Will. Most every philosopher, religion and perspective on life talks about man's inner compulsions to "miss the mark" by causing harm to himself, to others and falling short of any system of moral obedience. To some degree, all of us believe that man has the ability to "pull himself up by his bootstraps" and overcome some of our bent toward evil by education, self-discipline and religion. But, life and history also reveal that this "bootstrap idea" has serious limits, proving to be an utter failure in the long run. Individuals are overcome by their own raging demons, such as addictions to drugs, sexual perversions and decadent materialism. Marriages fall because of unfaithfulness, self-centeredness and pride. Governments become corrupted from within. Warring countries conquer other countries due to an unbridled lust for power.

The Gospel of Jesus Christ says, "There is no one that seeks God" - perfectly, continually and consistently – and that "all have sinned and fallen short of the glory of God" (Romans 3:23). This singular truth could only emanate from the mouth of our holy and awesome God, and it's one of the reasons why I believe the Gospel to be true. *It's assessment of sin is real* and propels one to see the absolute need for salvation…which Jesus as Messiah provided for us.

Christ Died To Redeem and Restore Our Relationship With God

This last truth of the Gospel is the only sensible solution to the problem of sin. Man's goodness is **not** good enough, his education **not** enlightened enough, his intentions **not** deep enough and his moral fiber **not** strong enough to love God and his fellow man. Someone or something from the outside must intervene and enable him to overcome his sinful bent, if he is ever to please a holy and righteous God. Because of this, God intervened in history and sent his only Son, Jesus, as a perfect, substitutionary sacrifice for our sin. Only faith in him can wash away our guilt and provide us with lasting and eternal peace with God. This is the Gospel, and it is the only trustworthy and *fundamental* understanding of life to be found.

So, in summary of these first three chapters…God exists. Indeed, he *must* exist logically, scientifically and in every other way. Secondly, evil also exists, although it has marred God's perfect creation, enabling disease and death to rule as well as causing man's separation from relationship with God. Thirdly, The Bible is the accumulation of God's prophetic and propositional truth for mankind. It is reliable and trustworthy as an historical record and unashamedly conveys the Word of God. Fourthly, the Bible's message is that Messiah Jesus came to this earth at the bequest of his Father to die in place of us, to bring forgiveness, and to restore an intimate relationship with Him. This gift of grace and mercy is specifically available for those who would believe in him and receive him as their personal Savior and Lord. Those who reject this message, will suffer the consequences of eternal punishment and separation from God for all eternity. All of these truths tell me that the God in whom I believe is the God who *is*.

Your Spiritual Tool Box

Today's Project:
Have Confidence In The Gospel

Your Blueprint:
"For this reason, I kneel before the Father, from whom every family in heaven and on earth derives its name. I pray that out of his glorious riches he may strengthen you with power through his Spirit in your inner being, so that Christ may dwell in your hearts through faith. And I pray that you, being rooted and established in love, may have power, together with all the Lord's holy people, to grasp how wide and long and high and deep is the love of Christ, and to know this love that surpasses knowledge—that you may be filled to the measure of all the fullness of God." (Eph. 3:14-19)

Keeping It Plumb:
The Gospel message is the only rational, realistic and responsible answer to man's spiritually broken situation. Nothing else seems to offer any sensible explanation for the human situation. Ultimately, however, a person must come to grips with the Gospel of Jesus Christ. Is it true, or is it false? I believe it to be true for many reasons, but fundamentally, because of the inherent truth in the *Gospel message itself*. It just "rings undeniably true" about who God is, about our sinfulness and separation from him, and about our need of a Savior.

Our Core Conviction

     It was a great day to be climbing and John was greatly skilled at it. He lived in the rural, mountainous country to the west of Denver, and today he was "raring to go!" He grabbed his gear and ran out the side door of his garage toward the woods. After about an hour's hike, he came to a place where small hills began to change into mountainous terrain. He peered upward at a particularly large ravine coming down from the top of a smaller mountain, about a 1500' high. The clouds seemed to be hanging a bit lower than usual, but for a fall day in late October, he couldn't complain. So, he began his climb.

     It took about another hour to get to the top, but the view was worth it, he said to himself. The little town where he lived was nestled down below on the other side of the forest. All the leaves had turned, so it was a palette of color across the wooded landscape.

     Suddenly, his left foot slipped and sent him sprawling down the short brush that lined the top of the ravine. He rolled through it all until he was just able to grab onto a fairly strong bush at the top, but his body was completely over the edge. He was hanging on for dear life, as they say…literally.

     "Help…help!" he shouted. But, no one answered.

     "Help…I'm falling…please…help me someone!"

Time passed. Finally, exhausted and hanging on after 30 minutes, John gave out one last yell. *"Help...please, somebody up there...help me!"*

"Do you believe?" came a deep and thunderous voice from above. John was dumbfounded, for no one was around that he could see.

"Do you believe?" came the same question again, seemingly out of the clouds. John said the only thing he could think of, assuming the voice to be the voice of God.

"Yes, of course, I believe!" he shouted up at the clouds.

"Let go of the bush," came the reply without delay. John looked down at the ravine with its jagged walls and huge boulders at the bottom. He paused, then looked up to the clouds again and shouted, *"Is there anyone else up there!"*

For the genuine believer, there's just isn't anyone else. He or she has to hang on to faith no matter what the difficulties or trials may be. The love of God in Jesus Christ is simply all consuming and too wonderful to either ignore or reject. Faith is such a life changing conviction that he or she simply refuses to turn back...perhaps a bit compromisingly at times, but ultimately always moving forward. In fact, it is John the Apostle that encourages us, knowing that only disingenuous followers turn away, thus showing their true natures.

> *"They went out from us, but they did not really belong to us. For if they had belonged to us, they would have remained with us; but their going showed that none of them belonged to us."* (I John 2:19)

Much of life has to do with what we believe...about God, about morality and about life in general. As said previously, deeply held convictions can change our lives. Often, people who have experienced and overcome significant personal problems, for instance, go on to start successful rehabilitation programs to help others. People with traumatic life experiences, like surviving a horrendous drunk-driving accident, will afterwards speak loudly in their condemnation of the causes that got them into trouble. I also find that people coming to Christ from lifestyles that were dramatically self-destructive tend to be less vacillating or compromising in their walk with Christ. Such folks have a deeply embedded conviction about the destructiveness, hopelessness and sinfulness of their previous lifestyle, which is why they seem so unwaveringly committed to him as Savior and Lord.

Perhaps most of us didn't come to Christ from "wildly sinful" backgrounds, but were raised in Christian homes, attended Christian colleges, etc. However, I've found that believers with this type of background seem to toy with sinful indulgences too easily, until stung or hooked by some sort of sin. If they realize the danger soon enough, they escape, but if not, they too find themselves caught in a sinful behavioral web. I think it's because they didn't have much experience with the hopeless and addictive side of sin before they came to Christ, so they of necessity have to learn about it...almost as naïve little children...before they are willing to stay focused and faithful to the Lord. Here's an example.

The internet – it's a dangerous playground, but it's quite capable of smacking a young, naïve believer in his spiritual face with temptation and sinful pitfalls. My MSN opening page always presents me with hundreds of sub topics to search, many of them nothing but unending, eye-catching, innuendo-trolling advertisements that jump out at me. All of them are creatively stuffed with colorful and attractive hooks designed to gain my attention. Such things are rarely just harmless parades of interesting facts and events. They are often deep swamps of sensual and/or sexual entrapment. So, if surfing, let's at least beware of the sharks!

But, my point in this chapter is for us to realize that we, as Christians, have at the core of who we are, a deeply embedded, core conviction of the Gospel of Jesus Christ. That core belief is something driven deep by God's indwelling Spirit, but it can be sabotaged by Satan and sin. Keeping it firm and unyielding is a critical and *fundamental* key to spiritual success.

Maintaining A Strong Core Faith In Christ

It is always the Gospel itself...its basic truths...that keeps our core faith alive and well (we defined the Gospel in the previous chapter). For a moment, let's consider a huge oil drilling rig built and maintained in the Gulf of Mexico. Many are fixed rigs, sending concrete and steel pinions deep into the sea bed in order to provide structural stability in all kinds of weather (water depths of around 2000'). There are also other kinds of semi-flexible rigs designed

(https://en.wikipedia.org/wiki/Oil_platform#Fixed_platforms)

to function in off shore waters around the world (in 12,000' water depths). One of the largest offshore platforms is the Hibernia platform in Canada, located in the Atlantic Ocean off the coast of Newfoundland. It's 364 feet high, weighs in at 1.2 million *tons,* and can withstand the impact of an *iceberg.*

The structure of such large oil drilling rigs always relies upon it being built and fixed to the ocean floor. The Gospel, and its truths, is our ocean floor. If we want to be safe from spiritually bad weather (from within or without), we must secure ourselves to its solid, immovable and fixed truths in the following way:

*Because I believe in Jesus Christ,
I will obey God in spite of all…no matter what.*

Again, our core faith is a *conviction*…a belief, an impassioned perspective, something strong and deep enough that all obstacles that oppose it must be kept subject to its realty. As we mature in Christ, everything we think and do should be measured by this spiritual yardstick. Every doubt that crosses my mind, every desire that opposes my obedience, every attitude that frustrates my commitment, and every habit that trips me up…all must eventually bow down in surrender before the glorious person of Jesus, the Son of God and our personal Savior and Lord.

The rest of this book is written *to build upon this fundamental conviction*. By way of example and as I mentioned before, when I was about 10 years old, my father purchased 6 wooded acres of land with an old, pine-boarded cabin in the middle of it. After we tore down that old cabin, I remember clearly how we dug an 8-foot-deep hole in the ground over 50 feet long and then lay cement brick walls within it for the foundation of our new home. It was a slow and methodical task, laying one grayish, 60 lb. cement block upon another. We'd stop and measure each block to be sure the line of bricks was level. Then, we'd grab another brick, throw some cement on top of the previous one, and slowly position the new brick on top of it. When we finished each side wall, I'd sometimes pause to admire our work (I only helped my uncle, the brick layer, carry the bricks). The wall, when finished, was impressive to a little guy like me, because it didn't just happen by a truck pouring cement into a mold…the wall was built *step by step*. It also involved a lot of other things, too, that had to be done correctly, if one wanted a straight, smooth, and level wall. Each thing you did, piece by piece, step by step, contributed to the sturdiness and longevity of those walls and the house itself.

If you've done this before, however, you'll understand that the walls are only the second part of the foundation. It's the "footing" that comprises the bed rock upon which the walls are laid. Because most houses aren't built upon a rock layer in the ground, something strong and immovable has to be laid first to hold the bricks firm and stationary. Again, that's the role of what builders call a footing, and it's laid along the entire outline of the foundation…poured, hardened concrete about four feet deep and eight to ten inches wide. Bricks are then laid upon that footing, upon which the wooden structure eventually rests. *Spiritually* speaking, our foundational footing is that statement I made above:

Because I believe in Jesus Christ,
I will obey God in spite of all…no matter what.

Now, if a foundational footing is done right, it won't shift over the years and the walls will be straight and sound. Similarly, if our faith is grounded correctly into our soul, a firm trust and a sincere commitment will hold us securely in Christ. We'll be welcomed into heaven while listening to Jesus' words of encouragement, "Well done, good and faithful servant."

Now, over the years our spiritual footing can be severely stressed by sensual temptations and Satanic erosions. And, every so often a piece of it may shift just a little, perhaps even chip a bit, because of an overgrown and protruding root. But, as believers, we just dig down, pour some fresh concrete from the Word of God and firm it up, with the Holy Spirit's guidance. It may not always be a simple process, and it may involve re-adjusting to God's blueprint and time-table for spiritual construction, but it will happen. We've got a fantastic carpenter, you know!

Your Spiritual Tool Box

Today's Project:

Always Believe

Your Blueprint:
"And without faith it is impossible to please God, because anyone who comes to him must believe that he exists and that he rewards those who earnestly seek him." (Heb. 11:6)

Keeping It Plumb:
There are many "survival situations" in life that one can find hard to endure, difficult to explain and challenging to one's commitment. Let faith be your compass and God's Word your map. Many have gone before you and succeeded, and not a one of them has ever been let down by God. Just keep on trusting in Jesus and *in Who He is!*

Your Framework:

Mental Management

Genuine conviction about God and his Son, Jesus, means that our lives will be changed by his indwelling Spirit from the point of salvation forward. Thus, the process of sanctification then emerges as our prime and ongoing responsibility. Our lives will be gradually transformed into more Christlike attitudes and behaviors. According to Romans 12:2, this process is fundamentally a mental process. Let's look at how managing our thought life is critical to our spiritual success.

Building Tip #1:
Always Be Watching!

In review, convictions at their core are deeply held and life-changing beliefs. The key belief for Christians is our belief and trust in Jesus as Savior and God. Many of the things we've discussed so far are simply buttresses to this essential platform of faith conviction and commitment, and that's why we've looked at these first. This Gospel faith/commitment is our fundamental position before God, and it provides intimate relationship with him...let's call it our **Consecration.**

> *"Therefore, I urge you, brothers and sisters, in view of God's mercy, to offer your bodies as a living sacrifice, holy and pleasing to God—this is your true and proper worship."* Romans 12:1

However, consecration is more than this...it's also an *ongoing process* as well. We've got to *practice* consecration with consistency, for our hearts tend to wander as sheep, loosening their grip on belief and commitment. God doesn't reward lazy or disobedient believers with spiritual maturity unless they *follow* the Holy Spirit's promptings within their minds and hearts. Therefore, genuinely consecrated believers realize they must *continue* to believe and to "re-consecrate" themselves daily in order to stay in right relationship with God.

The process of maintaining our consecration is helped by understanding how our inner person functions. Then, we can better target our daily responsibilities and spiritual goals for our ongoing relationship with Jesus Christ. I want to focus our attention on this for the next three chapters.

I understand that the New Testament essentially identifies three innate functionalities of our inner person. Here are the three functionalities:

1. **Watching** (ie. intellect, belief, logic, knowing, wisdom),
2. **Wanting** (inclinations, desires, emotions, feelings)
3. **Willing** (intension, determination, commitment, choice).

These "parts" or capacities interrelate with each other, just like a composite milkshake is made by mixing vanilla, chocolate and strawberry ice creams. All three are there and have specific functionality, but we cannot separate them with any specificity, other than in these three fundamental and obvious ways.

In this chapter, I want to focus upon the "watching" part of our inner person, which primarily involves maintaining a mental outlook pleasing to God. Like the look-out sailor on top of modern day warship viewing the oceanic horizon for the enemy, our spiritual eyes must stay focused in order to avoid any approaching marauders to our faith. Similarly, any building project needs a good "lookout" or construction manager to keep things moving and make sure that everything is being done right and in alignment with the blueprint. This is the role of our ***minds***.

"Do not conform to the pattern of this world, but be transformed by the renewing of your mind. Then you will be able to test and approve what God's will is—his good, pleasing and perfect will." Romans 12:2

My family lived in Massachusetts for a while, south of Boston, and in an area where it was common to find cranberry fields growing. These tasty berries were found on bushy clumps laying near the ground, which thrived in large fields that needed to be well-watered. If you walked through one of them, it just appeared to be low growing shrubs a foot or less tall. But, if you looked more closely, the cranberry shrubs were larger and deeper, having channels of water all around them. On closer observation, there was also a gated inlet stream flowing from a pond nearby, which allowed the water to come in at various times, depending, I guess, upon the farmer's wishes for harvesting purposes. I would assume that how he managed that waterflow was critical to the health of the cranberry crop.

Similarly, managing the flow of our minds is an important spiritual responsibility and a critical process for believers, if they are to reach any level of spiritual growth.

It's interesting that our minds have inherent abilities quite unique among all of God's creation. We look at life as it impacts us and make immediate interpretations of what it all means, as well as how to respond...all in a fraction of a second. Look at how fast, for instance, our minds process information.

> *"Neurons are **nerve cells** that process and transmit electrochemical signals. Like a little lightning bolt transmitter/receiver/processor. The human brain has about **100 billion** of them. Each neuron fires about **200 times per second**, and each neuron connects to about **1,000 other neurons**. So, every time each neuron fires a signal, 1,000 other neurons get that information. That's **20,000,000,000,000,000** (20 million billion) bits of information transmitted per second."*
> http://thephenomenalexperience.com/content/how-fast-is-your-brain/

Remember that our intellect interconnects the other functions (wanting and willing) letting us understand and relate to what's going on inside and outside of us. The mind "thinks," but it's conscious content varies at different times. So, at one time our thoughts are filled with passion, while at other times our thoughts may be just cold logic, and at other times our thoughts may be quite intentional. Overall, when all three of these capacities come into alignment, powerful *convictions* are formed and behaviors result...good or bad. You can see, therefore, that the flow and content of our thoughts is critical, when adjusting our lives toward the will of God. Okay, practically speaking, how do we use and/or manage our thoughts for effectively loving and serving God? Mental management is achieved in two ways.

First, we must learn to **Discern** (to *understand* God's Truth in Scripture and in life). We must ultimately accumulate a spiritually sound, mental library of beliefs (of which our faith/commitment is just one) and nurture these godly perspectives and attitudes into a healthy mindset.

> *"...this is my prayer: that your love may abound more and more in knowledge and depth of insight, so **that you may be able to discern** what is best and may be pure and blameless for the day of Christ, filled with the fruit of righteousness..."* (Philippians 1:9-11)

I had a cabinet maker friend by the name of Mike. Mike was a cop for a number of years, who retired and then formed his own cabinet building business. He would sit down with customers, ask them key questions about what they wanted in their kitchen layout, for instance, and then proceed to put it into a workable blueprint.

I remember him telling me that the one thing he hated the most about his business was when a customer would stroll through to see how things were coming along and then suggest something he or she would like *to add.* Now, when this happened, Mike often felt like responding with, *"Look, bub, this is how you laid it out and approved it, so don't try and change it now. Didn't you understand that I can't change the blueprint at this point? Are you crazy? Do you know how much time and added cost it will be just to make that one change?*

Well, that's how he felt, but I don't think he ever quite said that to a customer. He usually had to lose some profit just to please those customers who came up with such "last minute bright ideas!" By application, God's "unchanging" blueprint is found in the Word of God. Therefore, we must *discern* Biblical Truth, *remain focused* upon it and *stay in obedient commitment* to it in our daily lives. In other words, we must acquire and apply godly perspectives and spiritual attitudes.

> *"Behold, you delight in truth in the inward being, and you teach me wisdom in the secret heart..."* (Proverbs 13:14...ESV)

Understanding truth and godly perspectives as found in the Scriptures (and life), is a fundamental part of Christian living. It keeps us on the right track for God.

> *"...the fear of the Lord, that is wisdom, and to turn away from evil is understanding.'"* Job 28:28

For example, here's some godly beliefs, which, when added to faith, will keep us inwardly strong and outwardly obedient.

- **Trust**...I believe in God's ability to keep me safe and to provide for me and my family according to his perfect will.
- **Hope**...I rest comfortably in the assurance of heaven and in spending eternity with Jesus and others who have walked with him.
- **Purity**...I keep my mind set upon the things of Christ and the plan he has for my sensual and sexual needs.
- **Contentment**...Because I believe in eternity with Jesus, I am at peace. I focus upon *using* material comforts instead of *being used* by them.
- **Achievement**...Whatever plans I make or goals I choose, it is firstly the will of God that I will pursue, without greed or pride.

Acquiring understanding, knowledge, and wisdom is the first responsibility of the mind. Unfortunately, I know a lot of people, who are very knowledgeable, but not necessarily very wise. They are a storehouse of facts and information, but not necessarily anyone to go to for spiritual counsel. People with wisdom are people of understanding. They connect the factual dots in such a way as to bring benefit and helpful insight to someone. But, *Discerning* God's Truth is only half the battle!

 We also need to **Discipline** our minds in God's Truth, carefully monitoring our spiritual library of perspectives and attitudes (of which faith is the foundation), focusing only upon thoughts that are pleasing to the Spirit. We have to consistently inspect our thoughts to be sure they're not being hijacked by fear, lust, pride, jealousy, doubt, anger, or other wayward desires and harmful emotions. Though this is not always an easy task, nevertheless, spiritual maturity demands that we develop just such a focused "mindset" under the influence of the Spirit. As I mentioned before, imagine a switch on a wall with "on" and "off" on it. Always be ready to push it in either direction, depending upon which is in line with the will of God.

Success in this aspect of our inner person requires the "wanting" and "willing" functionalities of our inner person to comply with the will of God, so let's review these next.

Your Spiritual Tool Box

Today's Project:
Think Right

Your Blueprint:
*"Have this mind among yourselves,
which is yours in Christ Jesus."* (Phil. 2:5)

Keeping It Plumb:
Thinking right is not an option for believers. There's so much mental garbage out there that all of us are bombarded daily with skewed and/or inappropriate thoughts. In addition, there's a lot of junk thinking that we dredge up on our own from within that clogs up our spiritual lives as well. Spiritual success demands that we control our conscious and cognitive mindset.

"Spiritual maturity hinges upon our ability to discern, hold onto and focus upon the strategic truths found in God's Word."

Building Tip #2:
Always Be Wanting!

When we "think" about anything, our inner person may have pre-discerned patterns of thought lurking around within us as well, which can boldly invade our consciousness. Granted, sometimes our thoughts are just intellectual...with nothing attached, *but not always*. But, at other times, our minds can be viciously attacked by passions and/or emotions that can captivate our thinking and frustrate the inner workings of God's Spirit. It's a "good dog – bad dog" scenario.

Always Be "Wanting"

Little Susie May wanted to stand up and say something to her 3rd grade classmates. So, she jumped up out of turn to tell her summer story. But, her teacher told her to sit down and wait. After sitting down, it was quite obvious that she had gotten angry about waiting, her flushed cheeks pouting for all to see.

"Susie May, I didn't want to make you angry, but you just have to wait and stay seated, okay?" said her teacher as kindly as she could. But, Susie May wouldn't let it end there, so she looked up to her teacher and firmly responded.

"I may be sitting down on the outside, but I'm standing up on the inside!"

Similarly, many of us can't let go of our passions at times, though we may want to do so at the same time, oddly enough. Listen to the Apostle Paul for a moment:

> *"For we naturally love to do evil things that are just the opposite from the things that the Holy Spirit tells us to do; and the good things we want to do when the Spirit has his way with us are just the opposite of our natural desires. These two forces within us are constantly fighting each other to win control over us, and our wishes are never free from their pressures."*
> (Gal. 5:17 TLB)

Spiritual maturity demands that we learn to deeply *want* to love and obey God, regardless of all competing desires and tendencies to the contrary. For instance, a person of faith *wants* to love and serve God more than he wants to indulge his flesh or serve Satan. Now, this is an ongoing war as Paul mentions above. But, it is a *fundamental* struggle that must be consistently won at the level of trust and belief, if any believer is going to be successful and effective for Jesus Christ. In other words, our intellectual faith *must transform itself into inclinational faith as well*, or it will not move us toward ultimate obedience. Genuine faith conviction always inspires strong spiritual desire.

But, how do we move into the inclinational arena successfully? Again, God's Word and God's Spirit work together to plant spiritual desires into our minds and hearts. I have a plant in my living room that I originally got from my workplace. It's about 2 feet tall, prickly green, and has three independently growing stalks. Between my wife and myself, we try to keep it well watered, but both of us frequently forget to do so. Anyway, when all three stalks are watered evenly, each grows taller with consistency. But, when one doesn't get enough water, one can tell such is the situation, because the stalk dries up, becomes brownish in color, and hardens. Without attention, the stalk will eventually shrivel up and die.

As believers, it is a *fundamental* requirement that we drink in enough spiritual water on a regular basis to keep us healthy. Essentially, our resource is the Spirit of God, who provides his strength, his love and his merciful grace to us in a variety of helpful ways, the most important of which is the Word of God. The Spirit infuses his powerful resources into us as we study the Scriptures, fellowship with other believers, have Christian friendships, listen to godly preaching and/or teaching, enjoy Spirit-filled music, and offer genuine worship. Notice that by directing our mental focus upon the Word of God in these various areas, we receive the Spirit's empowerment from within.

> *"Let the message of Christ dwell among you richly as you teach and admonish one another with all wisdom through psalms, hymns, and songs from the Spirit, singing to God with gratitude in your hearts."* (Col. 3:16)

Wanting God and his Will for our lives is something that has to be cultivated within by God's Spirit. Did you know that the Holy Spirit is our enabler? Did you know that trying to increase your desire for God, in order to overcome lust, pride, anger and other fleshly desires, only comes through his resources and from his Spirit? Attempting to live for God and to desire him deeply can't happen without the Spirit's enablement, primarily, as we've said, through ingesting God's Word with consistently.

Listen to several selected verses from Psalm 119 as the Psalmist praises God for his Word. It's the longest psalm in the Bible, and it powerfully expresses the ability of God's Word to change our hearts, strengthen our wills and enlarge our understanding of God and his ways.

I have stored up your word in my heart,
that I might not sin against you…v11
Your testimonies are my delight;
they are my counselors…vs. 24
My soul melts away for sorrow;
strengthen me according to your word…vs. 28
I will lift up my hands toward your commandments,
which I love, and I will meditate on your statutes…vs. 48
My soul longs for your salvation;
I hope in your word…vs. 81
Oh, how I love your law!
It is my meditation all the day…vs. 97
Through your precepts I get understanding;
therefore I hate every false way…vs. 104
Your word is a lamp to my feet
and a light to my path…vs. 105
Your testimonies are my heritage forever,
for they are the joy of my heart…vs. 111
You are my hiding place and my shield;
I hope in your word…vs. 114
The unfolding of your words gives light;
it imparts understanding to the simple…vs. 130
My tongue will sing of your word,
for all your commandments are right…" vs. 172

When I go to a smorgasbord type of restaurant, it's fun to go up and down the salad and main course bar to see what might grab my culinary interests. There's the Italian type food, perhaps spaghetti with sausage, the thick layered lasagna smothered in ricotta cheese, or some huge beef raviolis. Next down the line is a selection of tender pork chops and chicken thighs, with choices of rice pilaf or creamy mashed potatoes. Next, slip on down to the server at the end. and he can slice off some succulent roast beef or a juicy cut of country ham. And, then there's the dessert bar...let's not even go there, okay!!

Is it my purpose to make your mouth drool and your appetite explode such that you run right out after reading this to the nearest buffet and indulge yourself without control? Not really...I just want to demonstrate the power of suggestion. In a similar way, our minds recall vivid snapshots of things we have enjoyed previously and can easily entice us by *re-thinking their pleasures*. The only way to overcome a sensual or serious "lust" in any form is to consider the privileges, purposes and pleasures of being a believer *in Jesus Christ*. We must fight fire with fire, in other words. "Wanting" anything engulfs the mind with desire, and if it's a sinful desire, we call it lust. Lust *can* be overcome by the Spirit, but *only* as we focus our heart desires upon what we want from God. Only the **deeper hunger** for spiritual purpose, for a rewarding ministry, for professional and family blessing, for good health from God, for peace of Christ in one's heart and for the certainty of eternal life...only these wants can overcome fleshly desires.

I would encourage you to tie a particularly meaningful verse to something you deeply want or enjoy in your relationship with God. Have several of these verses, dealing with specific areas of temptation you regularly face. And, when the moment of temptation comes, re-visit these verses and contemplate *how much they mean to you* and *why it is simply more important* to stay pure for God. The Spirit will then begin to move your heart away from the lust and toward your love for God and his will in your life. Yes, it's a process to learn, but it's also a powerful resource to build over time.

In summary, the *wanting* capacity of our being is stimulated by what is going on both inside of us and outside of us. Our mental focus must be controlled in such a way as to allow godly desires to flourish and to disallow evil desires from overwhelming our hearts (requires a yielded and committed will).

A wise, old-time preacher from the South gave this example of two bull dogs that he had tied up on a lease in his backyard. One was big and nicely behaved, but the smaller one was nasty, loud and would bite you if you got too close. A passerby asked him why the nice dog was so big.

"When I want the good one to grow, I feed it some mo' stuff. When I want the nasty one to grow, I feed it som' mo stuff."

"Well, the small one looks like it could use a good meal," said the passerby.

"Yup...I'm starvin' it this week, so it'll learn some manners!"

Sometimes spiritual manners demand drastic measures in order to keep out those nasty desires that bark so loudly in antagonism to the things of Christ. But, if we keep feeding the nasty dogs in our hearts, they grow up to bite us and the people around us. Feeding spiritual desires – the good dog - empowers God's righteous inclinations to grow within us. Such spiritual wants are enjoyable to experience and powerful to see exhibited in a believer's life. Let's always keep feeding the good dog "some mo' stuff," okay!

Your Spiritual Tool Box

Today's Project:

Desiring God

Your Blueprint:

"Rather, clothe yourselves with the Lord Jesus Christ, and do not think about how to gratify the desires of the flesh." (Rom. 13:14)

Keeping It Plumb:

Wanting God and his Will in our lives is our top priority...our *fundamental* spiritual goal. Developing this desire has to come from God in one way or another: The Holy spirit builds this motivation within us by means of the following:

1. Conscience: engendering moral responsibility.
2. Conviction: deepening personal accountability.
3. Consequence: teaching us through our failures to want God's will rather than our own.

- Spiritual maturity happens when we reach a level of life where we recognize that enjoying sin is too costly. The pleasure no longer justifies the pain, the spiritual loss is simply too great, the consequences too disruptive and the chastisement too severe to continue. We know we're not perfect, but on-going disobedience, pet sins and inconsistency are just no longer worth it.
- On a scale of 1 to 10 (highest), how high is your passion for God?

Building Tip #3:
Always Be Willing!

    This brings us to *willingness*. Impassioned belief (believing and wanting God's Will) has to be deep enough to move our will toward *commitment*. Now, this spirit of "willingness" does vacillate inside of us at times due to our sinful natures. But, it's still the determinative and decision-making part of our person, which must continually yield to the Spirit's voice above all other passions and purposes. It always steps out with Christ-like determination and resolve.

    Picture a lineman on a professional football team. He's up against some heavy and powerful linemen on the other side ready to hit him head on with all their might in the process of getting to the quarterback. How does he go up against a 300-lb. powerhouse of muscle and determination able to impose a bodily impact of 10 G's? Very carefully! Some of these hits have been recorded to impact a person with over 1600 lbs. of force (over 100 concussions are recorded every year in pro football). Commitment to use full impact power on the football field is not a choice, it's a necessity in order to survive!

    You might also picture that cranberry bog I mentioned above. It's time to flood the bog with water on a hot summer day, so the farmer goes over to the wooden gate at the entrance of the stream. The gate is only above three feet long and a couple of feet high, so one person can easily slide it up to allow the small, stream-filled pond to flood the field. So, he stands above it with legs planted and hands firmly grasping the wooden gate. He knows what he's doing, and he desires to do it, but is he willing? When he pulls that gate upwards, he proves himself "willing" and acts upon his impassioned conviction. Similarly, each day brings us opportunities to act upon our faith *conviction*. But, only those *"willing to lift the gate"* at any moment are truly people of genuine faith commitment.

I've taught men's Bible studies for years at my local church. One of the men shared a decision he had made, which helped him to move ahead in his Christian life. Apparently, he had a couple hundred DVD's that he watched routinely from time to time. However, some of them were pushing the edge of spiritual acceptability and some others, well, let's say they had simply fallen off the moral cliff. He finally decided that the better part of avoiding temptation was just throwing out the whole bunch…which he did! Now, that's a wise decision and a conscious commitment to do what pleases God. He "lifted the gate" of commitment to God's will by choosing to remove something contaminating to his spiritual mind and heart.

There's an older book written by an author named Harry Blamires called, "The Christian Mind." In it he warns that avoiding "Christian thinking" and commitments on the part of modern society will cause cultural disaster. He says the following:

> *"If the Christian mind does not sharpen itself to detect and expose what is bogus in moral attitudes and pronouncements at an early stage, one doubts whether any other force exists to check (this) disastrous drift…there is no ethical tradition in our midst sufficiently rational and logical to withstand the assaults of modern immoralists."*
>
> ("The Christian Mind," Harry Blamires, SPCK Publishers, London, England, 1966, Pg. 102).

Mr. Blamires prophesy has been fulfilled in today's culture. Our culture's determination to verbalize and outwardly acknowledge Christ's teaching has been emasculated in the name of PC culture. Moral discussions about God and Biblical teaching have been shoved back into the closet of "one's own beliefs," not welcomed into the marketplace of cultural thought any longer. Why? Because pluralistic society demands that we honor just about everyone's moral and religious beliefs…no matter what…in order to avoid offending another person. *Society would rather offend God's moral statutes as revealed in the Bible rather than offend a person's personal convictions!* All this points to what the Bible refers to as a "hardened" heart (or mindset). In Acts 28:27, God addresses this hardened *unwillingness* and *closed mindedness*.

> *"For this people's heart has become calloused; they hardly hear with their ears, and they have closed their eyes. Otherwise they might see with their eyes, hear with their ears, understand with their hearts and turn, and I would heal them."*

The above is a mind and heart that is **willfully closed** and **opposed** to truth. Jesus even referred to this on the part of some Pharisees as the "unforgiveable sin." It was unforgivable, because these Pharisees were rejecting the witness of God's Holy Spirit in their hearts with *finality* and *full determination*, so God "gave them up," if you will, to *their own choices*. He gave them the final opportunity to find forgiveness, but they decisively rejected it, thus sealing their own fate.

Now, as believers, this situation is not as hopeless as it is with those who have completely hardened their intentions in antagonism to the will of God. Yet, we still can be oppressed by Satan and overwhelmed at times by our own fleshly desires. This produces a hardening of our intentional commitment to Christ such that we "stray" from the straight and narrow path of spiritual priority and purity that God has laid out for us to follow. Again, *it always begins in our minds*, where we allow certain thoughts to flow into our consciousness. If not discerning and disciplined, such rogue thoughts can capture our desires and redirect our intentions toward sinful attitudes and activities for a season. Habits can form and lifestyles can be corrupted rather quickly, **if we fail to yield our wills in renewed commitment to the things of Christ.** We must be on *constant guard* against the onslaught of both subtle and/or substantial temptation, which seek to diminish our "willingness" to believe and serve God in holiness. Here's a true description of our how much sin cries out from within our broken hearts to serve itself instead of God.

> *"Sinful flesh is a smoldering fire that burns slowly, but intensely from within. It is untamed and immoral at its core, without conscience, compassion or cultural sensitivity. It thinks only of itself and can turn a wise man into a depraved fool in a second. It rationalizes evil, cohorts with compromise and corrupts all that is spiritually pure. When starved of its pleasure, it whines, complains and criticizes the truth, while rejecting all accountability or blame. It really is a restless rogue, ravaging the naïve and ran-sacking everything that resembles righteousness. Those that love duplicity and sensual degeneracy are drawn to its fantasies, not realizing that the cost for such indulgence may be exacted eternally."*

Our sin nature, along with its wayward intentions, is no toy to play with. Sinful desires can all to easily *captivate our attention* and *erode our willingness* to obey God. So, if your willingness to adopt the things of Christ into your life seems to have weakened lately and you are indulging sinful desires (little or large), remember what got you there in the first place…a weakened will and poor management of your mental capacities! It really isn't a matter of how great the outer or inner temptation was, for ultimately it is the willful choice of the sinner to embrace his or her sin. Yes, some temptations are stronger than others, which usually is the influence of previous mental choices. Nevertheless, the choice to stay pure and obedient to God's will rests with *our* willingness to stay true to the Christ, who gave up his life that we might have eternal life.

Here are some very relevant questions for us to consider regarding these three chapters given to managing our inner person.

- Do I seek God with a fully surrendered heart in the morning?
- How much do I really want the will of God in my life?
- Am I decisive or vacillating when spiritual temptation arises?
- Am I still *willfully* holding on to hidden areas of sinful tolerance?
- Do I have a "no-matter-what, in-spite-of-all" mindset focused upon God?
- Do I submissively pray like Jesus said: "Thy will be done…"

I hope these questions will reveal in you a genuine willingness and compliance to the things of Christ. But, if they are *convicting* to you instead, know that the Lord simply awaits the humble return on the part of anyone who has wandered away. We will forever fall short in different ways and at different seasons of our lives, of course, though this is never an excuse. It's just good to know that he is always there, awaiting our genuine confession and eager to restore our relationship with some needed mercy, grace and blessing! The words of King David are encouraging to all of us.

> *"I know my God that you test the heart and are pleased with integrity.*
> *All these things have I given **willingly** and with **honest intent**…"*
> (1 Chronicles 29:17)

Your Spiritual Tool Box

Today's Project:
Willingness Begins With Surrender

Your Blueprint:
"And you, my son Solomon, acknowledge the God of your father, and serve him with wholehearted devotion and with a willing mind, for the LORD searches every heart and understands every desire and every thought. If you seek him, he will be found by you; but if you forsake him, he will reject you forever." (I Chron. 28:9)

Keeping It Plumb:
David's idea of what willingness is all about is spot on. Willingness is not just "will power" or self-determination on the part of a believer to try and muscle up one's own strength to conquer sin (though we have a will and must use it). No, it's believing in Christ and wanting his will so much that we **yield** over to him control over our minds, our hearts, our feelings, our memories, our goals and our lives…in-spite-of-all and no-matter-what. Keep in mind that this is a process, and we vacillate as we grow up in it from time to time as we travel along our spiritual highways. That's where re-consecrating ourselves daily becomes an important roadside place to visit and refuel.

Willing is more than just determination.
*It's about **yielding** everything over **to God's will**.*

Your Furnishings:

Demonstrated Discipleship

The Christian life is a very practical life. Too often, I think, we believers tend to "over-spiritualize things," but Jesus never did. He outlined simple responsibilities in parables and teaching that, if you followed them, you would please God and move forward in your relationship with Him. Therefore, if the foundation to our spiritual house is faith, and the framework is mental management, then the furnishings are the inner and outer things we apply, which both show and legitimize our spiritual commitment to Christ.

Integrate Your Life

At our men's retreat about ten years ago, one of the guys got a hole in one at the local golf course, and he's been talking about it ever since! But, do you know how many he's gotten since then? Your guessed it, none! Now, that's not demeaning to his golfing ability at all for the odds of an amateur making a hole in one are not very good. Here are the stats:
- The odds of an <u>amateur</u> making a hole-in-one: 12,500 to 1
- The odds of a <u>low-handicapper</u> making a hole-in-one: 5,000 to 1
- The odds of a <u>professional</u> golfer making an ace: 2,500 to 1

By the way. that amateur above has to play at least 12,500 rounds of golf to do it at an average of about $50 per/game. He or she would need to spend $625,000 along the way and play 312 rounds of golf per/year for 40 years. So, luck favored my friend, for he's never played *that* much golf.

To be good a golfer one has to put many movements together accurately and repeatedly. It involves keeping the head down, the left arm tight and mostly straight, the legs slightly bent, maintaining a proper grip, following through carefully with the hips...and these are just a few of the basics. It can be a very frustrating game for those of us who only play once a week in the summer.

I say all the above to point out that the Christian life also involves repeated and consistent ***integration*** of many principles and spiritual tools necessary to manage our spiritual growth. Think with me about the following inconsistencies:
- Should one read the Bible regularly, yet seldom pray?

- Should one avoid actual unfaithfulness, yet indulge in sexual fantasies?
- Should one be highly moral, yet cheat on his income taxes?
- Should one disavow jealousy, but succumb to prejudice?
- Should one be spiritually mature, yet lack self-discipline?
- Should one enjoy personal worship, yet never go to church?
- Should one enjoy teaching, yet avoid sharing his or her faith?

Just as a professional golfer has been able to integrate into his swing all the important fundamentals necessary for success, so believers must similarly apply all the *spiritual fundamentals* necessary to bring spiritual success (e.g. maturity). Yet, it is so easy to be a lopsided believer, content and accepting of far too many "immaturities" and sins. This was one of my seminary's professor's (Dr. Ensworth) favorite topics. He often said, "Maturity can never be realized without having *all areas* of your life under construction and growing together in greater and greater consistency." Good advice!

By the way, this is not to pick on anyone or to be hyper-critical. All of us from spiritual infancy have had certain areas of personal growth that were either easier to control or slower to yield and be conquered...that's life, and God understands this. Recently, I got a phone call from someone in one of my Bible studies saying that one of the other guys, though not getting drunk for over a year, had slid back on the weekend. The tension of certain ongoing struggles got the best of him, and he ended up in the hospital, overcome by depression and alcohol. I called him the next day to encourage him, but he was especially bothered by the thought that God wouldn't forgive him. I mentioned that God's forgiveness is quick and assured, when one truly confesses something. Mostly, however, the battle is over whether or not *we can forgive ourselves*. He said to me later that God used that truth to really speak to his heart and bring healing.

So, spiritual maturity does take time, though certain things dog at our feet. We get lazy in some things, hyper in others. That's normal, but my point is only that *we shouldn't let it become acceptable.* We should "keep up the battle" and attack *on all fronts*, while never becoming lackadaisical and/or casual. The mission is critical and should never lose its intensity...complete, integrated and balanced spiritual growth! Here's some thoughts on how to better integrate our spiritual responsibilities.

> BE HONEST

No one else...not even ourselves...can put a definitive number on how mature we really are. But, we can easily pin-point how responsible we are to follow the disciplines we're supposed to be integrating into our lives. We know, for instance, if our prayer life is solid or if it's sporadic and characterized by shallow blurbs without much sincerity. We also know how often we enthusiastically sit down to study God's Word. Such attitudes and activities are either faithfully accomplished or they're not. So, *be honest* with yourself. God already knows anyway, so be truthful in your self-analysis and don't try to fool yourself, God or anyone else. Frankly, there's room for improvement in all of our lives.

BE REALISTIC

Some people get all nervous and guilty when they look at their relationship with God. That's probably good in the long run, for it keeps them from getting haughty. But, it's not good, when and if we move into the area of perfectionism. Perfectionism is:

> "...*flawlessness and setting excessively high-performance standards, accompanied by overly critical self-evaluations and concerns regarding others' evaluations.*" wikipedia.org/wiki/Perfectionism_(psychology)

Look, we're supposed to be moving ever forward in our moral and relational lives, because of our relationship with Christ...understood. But, we've got to leave room for our humanity, too, though this is never an excuse for sinning. The fact is that we do continually fall short of God's expectations, *so give yourself* some mercy and grace at times. You'll only frustrate yourself unnecessarily, if you're demanding yourself to *do everything right all the time.* Living in perfect harmony with the will of God is our absolute goal, but it's not a realistic expectation this side of heaven. All of us are going to frequently fail and trip over ourselves. The Apostle Paul says in Philippians 3:12:

> *"Not that I have already obtained all this, or have already arrived at my goal, but I press on to take hold of that for which Christ Jesus took hold of me."*

Can I suggest that if the Apostle Paul hadn't "arrived" yet, then either have you or I. So...be realistic about what's expected, while still pursuing godly goals.

BE GRACIOUS

In the rush to be fully committed and completely faithful to Christ, remember to be kind to others along the difficult path of maturity. It's strewn with a lot of pitfalls and rubble, and all of us stumble here and there. Some believers can be unnecessarily judgmental and condemning toward others' failures and struggles. We are in constant need of God's mercy and grace every day and so are others around us.

This is why Paul tells Dads, *"Fathers, do not exasperate your children; instead, bring them up in the training and instruction of the Lord."* (Eph. 6:4) He does this to warn fathers that they can be too hard on their children at times, "provoking them to anger" unnecessarily, simply because they heap too much expectation upon them. Better to wisely set the pace in a reasonable manner, which *inspires* the spiritual athlete instead of *expiring him.*

> **BE SERIOUS**

In all the above, knowing that we are called to obey God in all things, be serious with your efforts to please him. No need to make excuses for our bad days, just pick yourself up, confess your difficulties and failures, then get back in the race. Keep going…keep running…keep praying…keep moving forward, and the Lord will be with you. Avoid goofing off or getting side-tracked for long periods of time, and always "keep short accounts with God," as someone has said. God rewards the faithful, not the perfect.

"The Lord is compassionate and gracious,
slow to anger, abounding in love.
He will not always accuse,
nor will he harbor his anger forever;
he does not treat us as our sins deserve
or repay us according to our iniquities.
For as high as the heavens are above the earth,
so great is his love for those who fear him;
as far as the east is from the west,
so far has he removed our transgressions from us.
As a father has compassion on his children,
so the Lord has compassion on those who fear him;
for he knows how we are formed,
he remembers that we are dust."
Psalm 103:8-14

Your Spiritual Tool Box

Today's Project:
Daily Growth

Your Blueprint:

"For this very reason, make every effort to add to your faith goodness; and to goodness, knowledge; and to knowledge, self-control; and to self-control, perseverance; and to perseverance, godliness; and to godliness, mutual affection; and to mutual affection, love. For if you possess these qualities in increasing measure, they will keep you from being ineffective and unproductive in your knowledge of our Lord Jesus Christ." (I Peter 1:5-8)

Keeping It Plumb:

Peter clearly outlines the process of Christian growth as learning to add key elements and principles to our initial faith commitment. As we do this, we will become more mature and also more capable servants to accomplish God's purposes. Our lives will be:

Stay Pure

Three cars ago, I owned a Chevrolet Malibu, which I used mostly for business. It was an enjoyable riding, mid-sized vehicle with great gas mileage... more than 40 mpg on the highway! One hot summer day, however, I had to pick up my five-year-old grandchild and bring her to school. Unfortunately, her carton of milk for lunch dropped on the floor of the back seat, and I didn't know it. Unaware of it, I dropped her off for school and then returned to my office.

Over the next few days, the car developed a strong, but undefinable odor in it. I tried to isolate where it was coming from...under the hood, something dead, or something spilled on the seats. I finally found that the culprit was that fallen milk bottle, which had hidden itself under the front passenger seat and dripped all over the carpet. I couldn't wash the smell out myself and even took it to a local dealership to get clean, but even they couldn't "clear the air." Finally, I traded it in...and I prayed daily for the poor person who bought it!

There are things in life that are antagonistic to our walk with Jesus, and which to the discerning have a smell of sin. It does take a degree of spiritual maturity to identify these "worldly" things, but to do so is a necessary and *fundamental* part of the Christian walk. Otherwise, our lives become tainted with the odor of inappropriate attitudes and behaviors. It is critical that we allow God to speak to us about this stuff and to correct the situation as quickly as possible.

SENSUALITY

Sensuality is usually a word referring to something carnal and evil, but it doesn't have to do so. Frankly, we've been created by God to *enjoy* sensual feelings and impulses. The need for food is sensually based, which is quite pleasurable to satisfy, when going out to Red Lobster or the Olive Garden, for example. However, when leaving such restaurants in pain and feeling just plain "stuffed" beyond reason, perhaps we've exceeded in a small way what God had in mind for hunger satisfaction. There are many other cravings/desires as well, including one of the strongest, the desire for sexual satisfaction.

The Israelite kings of Old Testament times really blew it here. They disobeyed God's directives regarding multiple wives and concubines, which created all kinds of problems for themselves. From David forward, they continued to follow the custom of worldly societies around them, which resulted in family issues, cultural issues, ruling issues, and, in general, the overall loss of God's national blessing.

The key is to fulfill our desires and needs according to the will of God for them, not in absurd over-indulgence, which only satiates the souls thirst for carnality. But, that's essentially what sin does, right? It's that corrupted part of our person that seeks to do what we want over and against the will of God. So, a fundamental approach to our sensually "obsessed" nature, is to exert control over it and keep oneself from carnal over-indulgence. In other words, we need spiritual **purity.**

SENSITIVITY

"...King Solomon loved many foreign women...from the nations concerning which the LORD had said to the sons of Israel, "You shall not associate with them, nor shall they associate with you, for they will surely turn your heart away after their gods." Solomon held fast to these in love...." (I Kings 11:1, 2)

Solomon was the worst abuser regarding this issue of purity, and he should have known better, for God gave him a particular gift of wisdom to rule the kingdom. That, however, is the difference...knowledge is factual and wisdom is applied learning. Even knowledgeable folks need to learn the truth through experience, which often involves significant failure.

Solomon's spirituality went south, when he decided to play both sides, primarily thinking he could maintain his political position through acquiring over 900 wives and concubines, many of them foreign. He tried to maintain worship of

Yahweh, while allowing his wives to worship their own foreign gods. Unfortunately, his pride *dulled his sensitivity to the Word of God over time*, and his family and the nation ultimately suffered for it. Idolatry and all kinds of accompanying evils filtered into the culture of Israel, forcing God to bring significant judgment upon his people along the way.

Okay...but, what about purity for believers living in the 21st century? I would suggest that a *fundamental* responsibility for all of us is to acquire a *spiritually sensitive mindset (unlike Solomon).* Here's what I mean.

Look Discriminatively

Our eyes are intricately designed instruments to view the world around us and interact with it in healthy ways. But, because of our inner weaknesses and tendencies toward evil, we must keep our spiritual focus spiritually clean and appropriately focused.

Life happens. That's something someone quipped, but it remains true. All around us, things are going to happen...some good, some bad...and we have to deal with it according to the will of God. We're going to see some things that are harmless, but also some things that can be quite dangerous. Imagine how a soldier reacts when seeing his buddy in a nearby foxhole get blown to bits. Such an image is hard to forget and is often a residual part of Post Traumatic Syndrome. In such a case, the soldier really doesn't make the choice, of course, to repeatedly see that horrible event. But, the pain that follows such a thing is emotionally embedded and may even require professional counseling in order to bring healing.

But, I'm also concerned about our choices to indulge an improper focus, when it's knocking at our spiritual door and enticing us feed it. That can happen as we lay in bed fantasizing or sitting comfortably in our living room in front of an improper program. It can happen in our relationships as well as in what we allow ourselves to read or watch in a movie. Our eyes are ingesting everything just as "life happens" around us. Filter it carefully and discerningly through your heartfelt love for God, or you could catch a disabling virus, bringing immeasurable spiritual harm.

Touch Carefully

Sensitivity demands a discerning touch, too. Touch can be a wonderful thing, as when you put an encouraging arm on the shoulder of someone who is hurting. Or, it's the pure and exhilarating experience of a husband and wife expressing love for each other in a romantic embrace. But, again, touch can mean reaching out to willfully embrace evil as well, either mentally or physically, even though one rationalizes that it's okay.

> *"Therefore, come out from among unbelievers, and separate yourselves from them, says the LORD. Don't touch their filthy things, and I will welcome you."* (I Cor. 6:17 TLB)

Not every non-believer is completely evil in their attitudes or actions, nor is every believer *perfectly pure* from evil, either. Having said that, wise believers stay at arms-length from unnecessarily close relationships with their non-Christian friends and acquaintances, for instance. Getting too close in friendship and social occasions puts *their* moral values up close and can easily entice us in the wrong direction. Careless disregard for this truth has put believers in positions they cannot handle. They get overwhelmed by some sort of temptation to say, see or do something in direct opposition to the will of God. And, their fall can be loud.

Yes, all of us attend the sports events at our kids' schools. We also attend occasional plays or movies, and we real books and newspapers. We may have a cell phone and search the web for information on occasion, as well. So, let's not be too rigid here. But, it's a different world out there in comparison to the way many of us have been raised. Today's teenager doesn't have to sneak out to an x-rated movie theater any longer to see porn. He or she can view it in glorious color on a cell-phone or computer. More than 50 % of Pastors have said they have had a problem with computer porn. If *they* have problems because of reaching out with *an electronic touch,* think of the temptation facing a teenager today.

Another problem of "electronic touching" is bullying. Social media contacts allow angry, jealous and marginalized kids (or adults) to reach out and hurt someone by saying something bad about them in social media. Or, they can put out sexually compromising pictures about someone they dislike. The possibilities are endless it seems for those who want to "touch" others in a harmful way. But, it doesn't mean that all electronic gadgetry must be thrown away. That often means we are only throwing out the baby with the bathwater, to use an old expression.

So, let's wise up, fellow believers, and be extra-careful about the contacts we have with people, technology and entertainment (especially regarding our kids!). Our spirituality must be of sufficient **sensitivity** to recognize evil (or probable evil) and follow the Spirit's urging when he says, "Don't Touch That!"

Hear Selectively

Music is huge in today's world. One resource counted more than 350 different types or genres of musical taste, along with common ones such as classical, country, hip-hop, bluegrass, rock, jazz, opera, honky-tonk, swing, pop, and alternative. It's most often the words associated with the music that can offend Biblical principles, but it can be both. Choose wisely when you listen, because by combining visual stimuli with music and words, sin can influence our lifestyle in subtle ways. It can alter one's moods and soften one's spiritual convictions, if imbibed without spiritual sensitivity. Are you willing to give up what sounds good, but is reasonably inappropriate or compromising?

Entertainment today demands self-discipline. Consider the media in general? What about talk shows? What about internet providers, who pop-up liberally biased and slanted news stories as soon as you go online? What about rabidly liberal professors at certain universities that shovel philosophical garbage into the minds of naïve college kids? What about political hacks and congressional fog horns with self-serving motives and liberal agendas, who are energetically seeking to turn this great nation into an amoral and socialistic nightmare?

Folks, it's unbelievable what's out there in the world of ideas. For instance, it's great that freedom of speech is still accepted, but it's being monitored, over-controlled and greatly abused by today's (2017) media moguls with devastating success. Fundamental concepts and principles planted in this country's historical underpinnings by our founding fathers have been severed in the name of multi-culturalism and ethnic diversity. So, be careful what you listen to on the one hand, while on the other hand be strong and vocal about the necessity of moral absolutes and *Christian* principles in law and society.

Let's end on a positive note about listening in general. One of the greatest joys in my life is listening to great sermons on radio or in person from men like Chuck Swindoll, Adrian Rogers, Chuck Smith, John MacArthur, James Kennedy, James MacDonald, Ravi Zacharias, and so many more.

Worship Leader Don Moen

Add to such teaching the musical and worship mastery of a Don Moen, and heaven doesn't seem so far away!

Of course, there will always be different styles and differing tastes among Christians. But, it is wonderful to see how God seems to give each new generation of believers, key speakers and worship leaders that can bring both his message and his joy into our lives. Let's keep our ears focused only upon that which is *excellent,* okay, and upon that which *best* brings honor and glory to Jesus.

Your Spiritual Tool Box

Today's Project:
Purity Is A Choice

Your Blueprint:
"Finally, brothers and sisters, whatever is true, whatever is noble, whatever is right, whatever is pure, whatever is lovely, whatever is admirable—if anything is excellent or praiseworthy—think about such things. Whatever you have learned or received or heard from me, or seen in me—put it into practice. And the God of peace will be with you." (Phil. 3:8-9)

Keeping It Plumb:

Purity is a choice, not just a result of something always innately corrupt. When our minds slip into salacious or self-indulgent fantasies, our thoughts become soiled with sin, often perpetuating dirty attitudes and behaviors as well. However, minds under the control of God's Spirit, have thoughts that lead to a clean and respectable lifestyle. A pure mind is a pure life.

Let Others Into Your Life

My favorite movie series has always been Star Trek, which sent Captain Kirk, Bones, Scotty, and Spock racing through the galaxies to encounter new life. From the beginning, they were an amazing team, each with his own character traits that drew you to them, and made the series so special. One really couldn't imagine breaking up that team. When they remade the series recently, those original characters were still there, each with their own inimitable style. Their character lives were inextricably connected in such a way that each one contributed to the other and again made the new series a must to see.

To an older generation, there was a host of "cookie cutter" westerns, which also drew countless kids to see the same familiar characters week after week. One was Roy Rogers (who in real life was a committed Christian and shared his faith in churches and at Christian events in the 40's and 50's). He and his wife, Dale Evans Rogers, used their media recognition in movies and tv to talk about the love they had for their Savior and Lord. Their celebrity life, however, was not always as ideal as most would think, for they experienced significant times of pain and loss as they share in their book, "Angel Unaware."

Another western favorite way back was, "The Lone Ranger." He and his trusted companion, Tonto, would ride into danger and defeat bad hombres where ever they would hide, shouting out "Hi-Ho Silver!" at the end of his show and then ride his white horse off into the distance. What a guy!

One *fundamental* principle of Christian life is the necessity of having others of faith around us for support and companionship. Captain Kirk always had Bones, Scotty, Spock and others around him to face interstellar worlds, while Roy had Dale, his dog, Bullet, and his famous horse, Trigger! Even the Lone Ranger had Tonto as a sidekick, right?

Unfortunately, too many believers think that they can live out their faith alone...fighting Satan alone, defeating that addictive sin alone, handling stress alone, having a successful marriage alone, raising problem-free kids alone, etc. In *real life,* not movie going fantasies, this is just not the case. Yes, some folks are stronger and wiser than others, but they still have seasons of great need, too. All of us can both *be of help* to someone else as well as *rely upon the help* of another person in times of personal stress or difficulty. Let's review several ways that this need for support from others manifests itself in our lives as believers.

The word for "church" in the original language means "gathering or congregation" of people. It's a gathering of those who have been "called out" from the world around them to assemble together with God in their midst. God's church is made up of folks who know Christ as their personal Savior and Lord. Jesus described the mission of the church as follows:

> *"Then Jesus came to them and said, "All authority in heaven and on earth has been given to me. Therefore, go and make disciples of all nations, baptizing them in the name of the Father and of the Son and of the Holy Spirit, and teaching them to obey everything I have commanded you. And surely I am with you always, to the very end of the age."* (Matthew 28:18-20)

The one imperative command here given to the disciples constitutes their responsibility after Jesus returns to the Father. They are to "make disciples." He explains the details of this mission as first "baptizing them" and then "teaching them to follow." The mission is, therefore, to...

1. **Share the Gospel** so that others may believe in Jesus as Savior and Lord (thereby becoming members of the true church), and then following it up by the symbolic rite of baptism.
2. **Teach believers** how to live faithful and obedience lives for God (as the pastors, elders and lay folks teach one another, encourage each other, and discuss spiritual responsibilities around the Word of God).

For my purposes regarding this particular topic, I want to focus on the second responsibility above. We'll discuss the other later on. So...*How does the church help believers to live faithful and obedience lives for God?*

It Provides Correction

One of the blessings that fellowship provides is *practical teaching* through its Elders, Pastors, SS Teachers, VBS Teachers, Small Group Teachers and others. Gifted men and women in various roles use their gifts to bring meaningful, enabling and doctrinally sound instruction around the Word of God. Without it, most of us would succumb to crazy ideas about God, salvation and Christian living. Here's an example.

I remember at age 16 working a summer, grounds-keeping job for the town. Three of us were out on the grounds of an estate somewhere in Connecticut, when this co-worker (my age) started telling me about his "church." He had long hair, earrings, tattoos, beads and all the rest of it to reveal his sub-cultural background. But, that wasn't the problem. The real issue was his insistence that my church was false, because Christ had come back in the form of Brother Julius and was living in Meriden Connecticut. He lived there with his wife (one of seven, forgot her name) who supposedly was the incarnation of the Holy Spirit. Apparently, the two of them announced who they were starting a small commune of about 300 people, all about college age, and all "social drop-out" types. No matter how hard I tried, I couldn't convince him of his biblical errors and spiritual naïveté.

Now, even as a teenager, I was safely and well-grounded in Scriptural doctrine. Sadly, Brother Julius did convince a lot of needy, lost and searching kids to follow him. I'm told that the commune eventually got involved with some sort of real estate scheme and, along with the inherent sexual immorality within the group, he eventually lost all credibility. I learned that this false messiah died at age 71 in 1996. (http://articles.courant.com/1996-07-30/news/9607300243_1_cult-followers-paul-sweetman)

We are all prone to doctrinal and practical teaching errors on a far lesser scale, particularly if we don't really take sufficient time to study the fundamentals taught in Scripture. That's why Paul reminds us of an important responsibility:

> *"Let the message of Christ dwell among you richly as you teach and admonish one another with all wisdom..." (Col. 3:16)*

It Provides Comfort

Comfort is another one of the fundamental blessings that fellowship provides. We've all been in situations where being alone is difficult, particularly when facing a hard battle against sin or personal loss. That's when we need to understand that our God is a triune God...Father, Son and Holy Spirit. His nature is relational and communicative, and he's designed us to be the same. This means that he wants us to go to each other, to talk things through and to find the grace to endure and to win the race against the flesh and Satan.

In all of Scripture, I would suggest that it is David who seems to best represent someone who had a close and satisfying *relationship* with the Lord. These verses from Psalm 23 say it well.

> The Lord is my shepherd, I lack nothing.
> He makes me lie down in green pastures,
> he leads me beside quiet waters,
> he refreshes my soul.
> He guides me along the right paths
> for his name's sake.
> Even though I walk
> through the darkest valley,
> I will fear no evil,
> for you are with me;
> your rod and your staff,
> they comfort me.

David learned early on that God was eager to have him rely upon his mercy and grace. He overcame wild animals as a shepherd boy and conquered mighty warriors as an adult. In everything he did, he called upon God for support and direction, finding God's bountiful resources available and overflowing.

So, we are relational creatures. We need relationship with God, and we have it in Jesus Christ. But, do you *also* have a circle of friends you can go to for help and support? Such a supportive group of people can save you a lot of pain and stress by listening and learning from their combined wisdom. They can also renew your courage and commitment with their encouraging support, while allowing you to feel enriched, when you are the one *helping them out.*

Fellowship comes in a variety pack, like those packages of little boxes of cereal you used to get at the grocery story. One morning you want corn flakes, the next raisin bran and the next, some sort of granola. Well, spiritually speaking, one week we may be in need of some sort of group support from a Bible study or Small Group, for instance. The next week, perhaps we need the closer support of a Christian friend, so we grab a lunch together with someone you trust. Another week, however, you may find that listening to some worshipful Christian music gives you a measure of grace to stay on track. Yet, another week may find you seeking some wise counsel from your Pastor regarding a key lifestyle issue in which you've been struggling. Whatever may be the case, God's grace is available through various means for finding the strength and stamina to win your spiritual races for God. By the way, fellowship isn't a wish, it's a command:

> "...not giving up meeting together, as some are in the habit of doing, but encouraging one another - and all the more as you see the Day approaching." (Hebrews 10:25)

It Provides A Sense of *Calling*

Calling is what I refer to as God's purpose for each of us within the body of the church. Each of us has certain abilities and strengths that God has given us in order to minister to the needs of others. But, not everyone has a clear grasp on what these strengths might be, because it's a learning process. So, stepping out to teach that 6th grade Sunday school class or filling in at the Men's Bible study is a good way to find out how God has enabled and equipped you. No one is left out, for everyone has some degree of responsibility in the church of God. Your Christian life will take on new meaning and purpose, and you'll always be happier, when you've involved yourself in the fabric of your church's ministry. Get involved and try out a few things, while praying for God's grace and direction.

Your Spiritual Tool Box

Today's Project:
The Body of Christ

Your Blueprint:
"...to each one of us grace has been given as Christ apportioned it."
(Ephesians 4:7)

Keeping It Plumb:
Are you an independent type of person, or one who enjoys and needs involvement with others? As a body of believers, the Bible stresses that we don't have an option here, for all of us should be involved with other folks in the family of God...helping, supporting, caring and mentoring them in the fundamentals of the faith. There's no room for arguing, fighting or jealousy, only loving support.

Master Your Fears

Saul was really not kingly material, even though he was clearly chosen by God to rule. It's interesting to note that he was first found hiding behind some luggage when the people came to install him as Israel's first king. Samuel knew he was the one to be anointed, but for some reason Saul was fearful of being chosen.

I believe this was Saul's inner weakness, even though he stood out among all the men of Israel as being tall and impressive. He certainly "looked the part" to all who saw him emerging from behind that luggage. But, later on, this bent toward uncertainty and personal insecurity got him into trouble. The first time was with David, where Saul became obsessed with David's successes as a warrior. Instead of honoring him and welcoming his leadership, he listened to an evil spirit and became jealously fearful of David. He spent years trying to kill him, but Saul's own son, Jonathan, came to the aid of David. Along with others, David was protected and eventually became the next king, a man "after the heart of God."

The second time, however, Saul was worried about how the people would feel, if he waited too long for Samuel to arrive at the battle field. Some of his army started to scatter in fear of fighting against the massive army of approaching Philistines without Samuel's presence. So, Saul offered the pre-war sacrifices by himself in opposition to the direct commands of Samuel. The response on the part of Samuel was quick and decisive.

> "You acted foolishly...you have not kept the command the Lord your God gave you; if you had, he would have established your kingdom over Israel for all time. But, now your kingdom will not endure; the Lord has sought

out a man after his own heart and appointed him leader of his people, because you have not kept the Lord's command." (I Samuel 13:12-14)

There are two *other* significant situations, where Saul was led by his own fearful uncertainty instead of by reverence for God. One was when he kept a part of the spoils of war for his own people, instead of killing everything that lived (I Samuel 15). In that case, he even lied to Samuel, when being questioned about his disobedience. When the truth came out, he was *afraid* of the people's opposition to destroying all the booty of war. The other situation was when Saul sought the counsel of a medium for help in another battle with the Philistines. God was not leading him or giving him counsel any longer, so Saul had her "bring up" Samuel from the dead in order to gain God's guidance. Saul was torn by fear, for as the Scripture says, *"When Saul saw the Philistine army, he was afraid; terror filled his heart."* (I Samuel 28:5)

We can see in the life of this physically impressive, but inwardly oppressed man, the unfortunate rewards of yielding to emotional fear. But, fear comes in many forms, and it can destroy you and I as far as living a peaceful and productive life for the Lord Jesus. According to a popular website, the following are the ten top things humans fear in order of strength. The worst is fear of failure, then in descending order follows death, rejection, ridicule, loneliness, misery, disappointment, pain, the unknown, and losing your freedom. (http://listverse.com/2011/09/30/top-10-strong-human-fears/)

It's interesting that most of these fears can be strategically and successfully faced by having a strong faith in the will of God. Worrying about what "might happen" is deadly, but developing a more in-depth understanding of the love that God has for us is calming and builds inner confidence.

"And we know that in all things God works for the good of those who love him, who have been called according to his purpose." (Rom. 8:28)

Let's look at another Biblical character, but who handled fear appropriately...David. As a shepherd boy facing a lion or bear, he relied upon God's protection, instead of giving in to fearful emotions.

"Your servant has killed both the lion and the bear; this uncircumcised Philistine will be like one of them, because h has defied the armies of the living God. The Lord who delivered me from the paw of the lion and the paw of the bear will deliver me from the hand of this Philistine." (I Samuel 17:36-37)

When encountering the insulting rantings of the giant, Goliath, as well as the awesome power of his Philistine army taunting the Israelites behind him, he did not cower, but offered his services. Goliath fell because of David's trusting obedience to Yahweh, when the whole Israelite army, and Saul himself, could not muster the same faith to fight boldly and confidently.

Years later, David faced the discouragement of losing his home base of Ziklag at the hands of the Amalekites. His men's families and property were stolen away, along with his own, yet, even then his fears did not consume him.

> "David was greatly distressed because the men were talking of stoning him; each one was bitter in spirit, because of his sons and daughters. **But David found strength in the Lord his God."** (I Samuel 30:5-6)

David had every reason to fear death and the loss of his promised kingship. Though depressed temporarily, his feelings didn't lead him into the depths of depression. He took control of them and redirected them toward the One who could do all things, and sought God's will. He went after the Amalekites and gained everything back after an impressive victory.

All of us must handle fear by making reasonably responsible choices for our own safety. I went to a Bible study once, where a guy seriously tried to tell me that seat belts, locks on doors and other protective devices were unnecessary for believers…God would protect you. In fact, having those things was not even acceptable, for it meant you were not trusting God. No amount of persuasiveness could move his stubborn viewpoint. I never heard what happened to him in life, but I bet he had some "eye-opening" experiences! If what this person falsely believed was indeed true, there would be no need for prayer, for wisdom, for police, or for national armies! His thinking was *presumptive* at best.

Let's be practical. All of us need to *apply* proper principles of wisdom by which to live. As we apply them intelligently, we will learn to conquer fear and have success in all areas of our lives. But, along the way, we *must trust* that God's loving oversight will be with us, and that his grace will guide us to make good decisions along the way. Making wise decisions and faith…that's the ticket to overcoming unwanted fear.

Proverbs is certainly full of such helpful and instructional bits of wisdom. Nehemiah, though, is probably the best example of a man who sought God and followed his will, but who also used common sense, discernment and wisdom.

> "But when Sanballat, Tobiah, the Arabs, the Ammonites and the people of Ashdod heard that the repairs to Jerusalem's walls had gone ahead and that the gaps were being closed, they were very angry. **They all plotted together to come and fight against Jerusalem** and stir up

trouble against it. **But we prayed to our God and posted a guard day and night to meet this threat...**Then the Jews who lived near them came and told us ten times over, "Wherever you turn, they will attack us." Therefore, **I stationed some of the people behind the lowest points of the wall at the exposed places, posting them by families, with their swords, spears and bows.** After I looked things over, I stood up and said to the nobles, the officials and the rest of the people, "Don't be afraid of them. **Remember the Lord, who is great and awesome, and fight for your families, your sons and your daughters, your wives and your homes...**From that day on, half of my men did the work, while the other half were equipped with spears, shields, bows and armor. The officers posted themselves behind all the people of Judah who were building the wall. Those who carried materials did their work with one hand and held a weapon in the other, and each of the builders wore his sword at his side as he worked. But the man who sounded the trumpet stayed with me. Then I said to the nobles, the officials and the rest of the people, 'The work is extensive and spread out, and we are widely separated from each other along the wall. Wherever you hear the sound of the trumpet, join us there. Our God will fight for us!' **So, we continued the work with half the men holding spears, from the first light of dawn till the stars came out.** At that time, I also said to the people, "Have every man and his helper stay inside Jerusalem at night, so they can serve us as guards by night and as workers by day." **Neither I nor my brothers nor my men nor the guards with me took off our clothes; each had his weapon, even when he went for water."** (Nehemiah 4:7-23)

Notice the practical blend of common sense, responsibility and prayerful trust that Nehemiah exhibited in God, and which we should follow. Doing so puts our minds to rest by focusing upon God's unconditional love for us, while we make responsible and cautious choices in the way we live. He's already aware of our thinking, our plans, our attitudes and our choices long before we even develop them...talk about the awesome power of Jesus, our Savior and Lord!

So, let faith occupy your mind and those fearful thoughts will leave. When you've reasonably done all you can do in any situation, allow God to be who he is...the sovereign, unsurprised, immovable and reliable protector of your life! Remember: Loving God completely will "cast out fear!" (See I John 4:18)

Your Spiritual Tool Box

Today's Project:
Peace and Quiet

Your Blueprint:
"Do not be anxious about anything, but in every situation, by prayer and petition, with thanksgiving, present your requests to God. And the peace of God, which transcends all understanding, will guard your hearts and your minds in Christ Jesus." (Phil. 4:6,7)

Keeping It Plumb:

Fear, anxiety, worry, etc., can pop up rather quickly in our lives, depending upon what's happening. And, along with challenges in the workplace and international tensions, a person can reach "overload" rather quickly and plunge into fearful reactions. But, Christ wants us to trust in his sovereign grace and purposeful oversight over everything that happens or possibly *could* happen to us. But, of course, it's that "possibly could happen" that usually gives us the most problems, right...fear of the unknown? The key to handling this is to trust in the one you do know...the Lord Jesus. He is omniscient, so nothing surprises him. He's omnipotent, so nothing can overwhelm or overpower his will. He's also eternal, which means that nothing can *ever, ever, EVER* surprise him or overwhelm him. Beyond this, *"in everything he's working for good in our lives." (Romans 8:28)*. So, let me ask you, "Is there really anything to worry about?"

Resign as the Master Designer of the universe ...the job's already taken!

> Our Father, who art in heaven,
> Hallowed by thy name.
> Thy Kingdom come,
> Thy will be done,
> On earth as it is in heaven.
> Give us this day our daily bread.
> And forgive us our trespasses,
> As we forgive those who
> trespass against us.
> And lead us not into temptation,
> But deliver us from evil.
> For thine is the kingdom, the power
> and the glory for ever and ever.
> Amen

Jesus, On Prayer

One can't sit at the feet of anyone better than the Lord Jesus, when learning about prayer. The "Lord's Prayer" has travelled the globe and continues to inspire all of us…and unbelievers as well…with its encouraging words and truths.

Of course, it is believers that truly have the hope and encouragement that it brings, because we have a relationship with God through his Son, Jesus. That relationship provides both *the right* and *the reason* we can expect God to answer our requests and needs. By placing our faith in Christ as our personal Savior, God has forgiven us for all our sin, bridging the gap that stood in the way of knowing and relating to God. Before we believed, that sinful condition separated us from God's beneficial kindness, protection and blessing. Unbelievers live estranged lives, alone and having no "atonement" for their sins. By believing in Christ, that relationship of love and harmony with God was restored. Just like Adam, we can now walk and *talk* with God without worry regarding his wrath over sin.

The Lord's prayer is more, however, than a beautiful symbol or saying that we learned in Sunday School. It's a profound prayer with meaningful truths about our relationship with God and how we should live. So, let's review some key points in it that he wants us to remember when praying.

First, a good way to start prayer is to praise and honor him for who he is...Almighty God, the Awesome Creator of the entire universe, of which we exist as a speck in time and space. How great is God and how immense is the power of his word to hold the universe together.

"Now faith is confidence in what we hope for and assurance about what we do not see. This is what the ancients were commended for. By faith we understand that the universe was formed at God's command, so that what is seen was not made out of what was visible." (Heb. 11:1-3)

God created the universe, just as if we were building a house or constructing a piece of furniture. But, by application, he also created the wood itself, which he used to fabricate the house or the furniture. In other words, he brought into existence the very physical structure of all that exists, using nothing before. This is the concept of the Hebrew word, *BARA*, translated "create" – out of nothing.

Scientists are still trying to understand the physical universe. Rather than just recognizing only 3 or 4 dimensions of existence, they now are conjecturing that there may be as many as *eleven* (according to the "M theory"). And, this doesn't even consider the spiritual dimension, which, according to the Scripture, is populated by a host of angelic and other beings. So, if it's too much to "get your hands" around, remember that prayerfully praising God recognizes our position in relationship to Christ, who is the creator of the very world around us and beyond. It should give us a proper sense of humility, when praying and seeking his blessing for our lives.

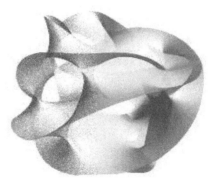
A theoretical quantum physics "string" representing 11 dimensions

Secondly, after acknowledging the almighty power and presence of God and his Son, we should immediately be struck by a profound sense of *submission* to his purposes for us and for the world at large: *"Thy will be done on earth as it is in heaven."* One doesn't come before this awesome God looking to shake hands with him as a friend or as a fellow creature. No...we should humbly surrender our hearts in obedience to his majestic person and perfect will for our lives.

A rather large and muscular man and his wife walked into the grocery store to buy a head of lettuce. He went away from her to check on something, while she went over to the produce department for the lettuce. She was a tiny lady and very soft spoken, but she approached a produce worker and asked, "May I have half a head of lettuce, please?"

"What!" responded the worker. "A half a head of lettuce…are you crazy, lady? We don't have any such things." The department manager happened to be rounding the corner about that time, so the worker started complaining to him about the lady's request.

"This is ridiculous, sir, this lady wants a half a head of lettuce!" Right behind the department manager was the lady's sizeable husband, who had also overheard the worker's angry, demeaning words. So, the worker quickly smiled at him and sheepishly responded:

"Oh…ah…yes, and this *fine* gentleman would like the *other half!*"

Amazing how a person's size can change a situation. But, imagine the immensity and capabilities of the One who designed the universe and who holds it in place. Ought we not to be submissive to his will, knowing that it must be as perfect and acceptable as his very being? Surrendering to the will of God in your daily prayers keeps our relationship with God where it should be. God is pleased when we *seek* him in prayer, but he is even more pleased when we *humble* ourselves before him in prayer.

Thirdly, we bring our requests to God for his blessing. Notice that we should be praying daily for our needs. In other words, praying to win the lottery may not be your best approach. Riches sometimes can be the biggest problem for someone, because they can easily lose the sense of necessity for God and prayer. A poor person struggles with blaming God, while a rich person struggles with ignoring him. Better to pray modestly and receive daily blessing.

Fourthly, we seek his forgiveness, while at the same time we forgive others who have sinned against us. There's probably not an hour in the day in which we have not somehow sinned in attitude or action. Confession clears any annoying and debilitating guilt from our hearts, quickly restoring the relationship to its purest intention. That's so critical, if the day is going to be all that it can be for Christ. It also suffocates all the seedling shoots of willful sin, which emerge in our hearts and minds. Then, in that same spirit, we *also* must sincerely give to others that *same* mercy and grace that we have secured through prayer. So, we confess any stubborn resentments and grudges we might be holding against them.

> "Therefore, if you are offering your gift at the altar and there remember that your brother or sister has something against you, leave your gift there in front of the altar. First go and be reconciled to them; then come and offer your gift." (Matt. 5:23-24)

Lastly, it's good to finish our prayers with adoration and praise once more. We've talked about humility, now we can thankfully rejoice in our eternal relationship with Jesus Christ, knowing all is well, even when the way may for a season be unclear. God's sight is never darkened, nor is the eyesight of genuine faith.

Your Spiritual Tool Box

Today's Project:
Pray Like Jesus Prayed

Your Blueprint:
"And going a little farther he fell on his face and prayed, saying, "My Father, if it be possible, let this cup pass from me; nevertheless, not as I will, but as you will." (Matthew 26:39)

Keeping It Plumb:

The Son and the Father lived in perfect harmony. Christ recognized that his one, overall objective was to please his heavenly Father, looking to him for daily provision and protection. He kept his eyes upon the loving care and purposeful oversight of the One whose love for him could never fail. Do you?

Breaking Bad Habits

  I was watching an intriguing program on the weather station the other day about "extreme weather." It's amazing how powerful the resident forces of nature are in hurricanes, floods and tornadoes. However, I wasn't aware of the significant damage that *hail* can do.

  In this story, two men driving along the highway out west were besieged by a dark, rain-gorged windstorm that suddenly turned to hail. These were not small bits of frozen water, but ragged chunks of falling ice the size of tangerines. These huge hail stones pummeled their car with welts and dents, finally taking out their front and rear windshields, before the two of them came to a stop. They tried to make a quick end run to an old farmhouse, but had to retreat back to the car for fear of their very lives. They came out of it alive, but were in awe of the destructive power of a hailstorm.

  Let's take a deeper look at sin for a moment. Strong, seductive habits are inclinations so deeply enrooted that they just blow past our will and pull us into disobedience. It may be a jealous spirit, a sensual lust, a critical attitude or any number of things. But, if we keep feeding it, it can grow into a nasty little storm, which dominates our lives. It often weights us down to a spiritual crawl.

There's a common background found in people dealing with sinful habits. They began by toying with some sort of sin, not very often, but on occasion. Gradually, an inclinational hook was planted within, and he or she mentally revisited the sin, then acted upon it more frequently. As the chain of impassioned thought tightened, the person became more mentally bound to repeat the unwanted act...with greater frequency, thus adding to his or her spiritual frustration

In your Christian life, be aware that not everything that's sinful in your walk with Christ is going to just "give up" like a bad guy facing the barrel end of a policeman's gun. Some things are very much ingrained because of the way we've been raised, the particular type of sin, and how many times we've repeated it. Bad habits are often difficult to break, but here's how to deal with such things with greater success.

First, *don't get involved with a repetitive sin in the first place!* This means knowing your weaknesses and wisely refusing to repeatedly do them. It's a simple answer, I know, but it's a lot easier to deal with any sin in the beginning **before** it becomes more deeply enrooted in your spirit. A habit is only increased by repetitive behaviors, so stop it soon before *fueling it with increased power.*

They say that marijuana is a gateway drug to heroine, sort of an easy connection that pulls one into harder drugs quite easily. In the same way, spiritually "soft sins" pull us quickly into "harder" sins rather quickly. For example, watching "soft porn" on television easily captivates a person into doing things like renting or buying porn...more of the raw and hard-core stuff. Another would be allowing a few explicative type words into one's vocabulary, which soon opens the door to increased diatribes of hateful speech, when overcome by anger.

> *"The prudent see danger and take refuge, but the simple keep going and pay the penalty." Proverbs 27:12*

Secondly, *fleshy type* habits are particularly nasty to overcome, because they usually *feel so good*...that's why we want to repeat them. So, to overcome a fleshy thought pattern, *try "thinking"* instead of *"feeling."* For instance, we may *feel like* getting high on something, or *feel like* having sexual gratification of some sort, or even *feel like* shouting back at someone. Continuing that "feeling focused" thought only gratifies and empowers it. Stop focusing upon that sinful thought or negative emotion immediately and, instead, focus upon something good or godly. **Grab** your mind and *yank it away* from mental sin and indulgence! **Re-focus your thoughts** upon a Scripture verse, a bit of wisdom or something positive, instead. In time, this will become a habit...the ability to *think right and stay focused* upon what is truly good and godly.

*"Rather, clothe yourselves with **the LORD Jesus** Christ, and do not think about how to gratify the desires of the flesh."* Rom. 13:14

Thirdly, pray. It's hard to stay carnally or emotionally focused when you bow your heart and ask God for help. Just getting your mind upon God and his Word helps initially for it momentarily severs the particular tie that's pulling at you. But, beyond that, God's Spirit works at redirecting our desires toward spiritually appropriate thought patterns as well.

Remember, though, that **we** are still involved in the process, and that necessitates a willing mindset, readily embracing a godly attitude or behavior. We are not robots and the Spirit is not a puppet master pulling behavioral strings without requiring us to make good choices as necessary.

In the book to the Ephesians, Paul teaches us that any of us can "frustrate" God's Spirit. Still, his inner promptings are sufficient and powerful enough to enable us to resist whatever habitual evil is pulling at us…*if we yield to his calling.* Much of this battle is a battle of ownership, which may take time and failure on our part before we come around in our mind, surrender our hearts, and let God be God over our lives. This also requires humility, for James 4:10 says:

"Humble yourselves before the Lord and he will lift you up."

Fourthly, *fill your life* with godly activities like serious devotions, Christian books and music, and attending activities at church. At the same time, *remove yourself* from the sources of your weakness. Avoid associating with people or places that bring temptation into your life. Always keep this bit of wisdom in mind:

"You'll be tomorrow, where you were yesterday,
unless you change today?"

Okay…*it's today*, so make the choices and changes you need to make, keep your focus and don't repeat the same sins. Albert **Einstein** said the definition of insanity is *doing the same thing over and over again and expecting a different result.* By way of application, Christians that expect spiritual growth cannot keep doing the same things that brings habitual failure into their lives…or they will *"still be tomorrow where they were yesterday."*

So, evaluate your personal prayer life, for instance, your fellowship depth and your mindset throughout the day. Also, are there small groups of co-strugglers in your church, where you can find support, wisdom and encouragement? Are there things you can do - activities, sports, lunches with friends, books to read, workshops to attend, etc. - which help to keep your focus upon positive things? Carry some verse cards with you available for quick access when you need them throughout your day. This really helps to break stubborn habits.

Lastly, seek godly counsel as necessary, for many folks have already successfully dealt with the very things you may be dealing with. Re-inventing the wheel, as has been often said, is entirely a waste of time and energy. A good friend can be a fantastic resource to a believer in need of knowledge and wisdom. Proverbs 15:22 says:

> "Without consultation, plans are frustrated,
> but with many counselors they succeed."

Overall, always be serious with your spiritual responsibilities. In that way, God will recognize the sincerity of your heart and begin to bless your efforts.

Your Spiritual Tool Box

Today's Project:
Break The Chain

Your Blueprint:

"My son, do not make light of the Lord's discipline, and do not lose heart when he rebukes you, because the Lord disciplines the one he loves, and he chastens everyone he accepts as his son. Endure hardship as discipline; God is treating you as his children. For what children are not disciplined by their father?.......No discipline seems pleasant at the time, but painful. Later on, however, it produces a harvest of righteousness and peace for those who have been trained by it. Therefore, strengthen your feeble arms and weak knees. Make level paths for your feet, so that the lame may not be disabled, but rather healed." (Heb. 12:4-8; 11-13)

Keeping It Plumb:

A person works hard at disobedience, and the result can often be binding habits that are also hard to break. God then steps in to bring significant discomfort and discipline, which seeks to revitalize the backslider's spiritual conviction through repentance (restoration of relationship). The process continues only as the believer gets serious enough to start out on a new path...a difficult one...but a pure and renewed walk with God (restoration of lifestyle). The only question in all of this is, "Will he or she respond to God's discipline and obey?"

"In matters of style, swim with the current; in matters of principle, stand like a rock."
Attributed by many to Thomas Jefferson

Avoiding Compromise

Most believers acquire moral issues in their lives because, though they start out fine, they begin to compromise and allow certain indulgences (usually small at the beginning). But, when anyone does this, his/her mind stores up images and/or fantasies that can suddenly pop up during the course of one's day. In the beginning, these things may be quite manageable, but if left undisciplined, they can easily demand more of our attention. We begin to have our own little world of lust, or pride, or jealousy or something else that compromises our commitment to Christ. And, compromise usually leads to spiritual trouble.

Joyce was a good mother of two, with a loving husband and a good track record of spiritual maturity. She lost her morning part time job, and it wasn't too long before she was trying to fill up that empty time slot with TV, while the kids were at school. She fell into the habit of watching a well-known soap opera and became somewhat obsessed with the plot line, which contained a lot of sexual situations and infidelity. Soon and quite subtly, she found herself being dissatisfied with her own marriage and home life. Her husband noticed the changes, but didn't understand why she was becoming so impatient and rejecting toward him. She even resigned as Sunday School teacher and VBS helper, in which she had been involved consistently through the years. After a few counseling sessions with the Pastor, she and her husband isolated the problem as stemming from the negative and sinful attitudes she had adopted over the months by watching that soap opera.

There's an account in the Old Testament of the prophet Elijah's encounter with Ahab, king of Israel around 870-850 BC. He was sent to Ahab to challenge and purify the idolatrous condition of the people, specifically because of Ahab's continual spiritual compromising. According to the Bible, *"...Ahab did more evil in the eyes of the Lord than any of those (kings) before him."* (I Kings 16:30)

The situation was that Ahab was "blending" Jehovah worship along with all the other kinds of idolatry within the nation of Israel. There were hundreds of these heathen priests/prophets, who were even invited to dine at the king's table on a regular basis. Over time, Baal worship actually became the ruling choice of Ahab.

Why did this happen? It happened because Ahab married a foreign woman by the name of Jezebel, who brought all her idolatrous gods with her. She tried to kill all the true prophets of God, but was unable to do so because of the courageous actions of Obadiah, who was in charge of the palace. He hid them from her murderous intentions. The people had a long history of idolatry anyway, but her control and influence over Ahab and the Israelites was devastating enough for God to eventually call Elijah to a "battle of the prophets" upon Mt. Carmel. Elijah, the servant and prophet of the Lord, won that battle over all the false prophets that challenged him (see I Kings 18).

Here's my challenge regarding all this. It is *fundamentally* important that we never blend inappropriate or sinful culture into the culture of the church (personally or corporately). Compromise is one of the ways the devil gets to weaken us slowly from the inside. For instance, consider a car salesman who will come down in price, while the customer comes up in order to close the deal on a new car. That's a *good compromise* for both the salesperson and the customer. But, bad things can happen when a believer compromises on his/her moral standards by giving in, backing off or loosening up on his/her Christian values in order to enjoy something, watch something, say something or hang around with someone he or she shouldn't be involved with at all. Compromise kills character by blending into it the values of a sinful world.

"I'll just watch a little of that TV program that's promoting sexual immorality."
"Awe, a little bit won't hook me. I'm able to say no, when I want to."

"Hey, I can't stop hanging around with Bill, just because he swears a lot." No one's perfect, you know."

"I know, I should be more into my devotional life. But, God will forgive me."

Now, we're not monks living in a solitary stone cave in Tibet. No, we're immersed in a society that has a whole lot of obvious and often subtle temptations riddled through it. Complete separation from the sinful attitudes and behaviors of others at work, at social occasions, or at entertainment venues is impossible. BUT, we can intentionally separate ourselves from *unwise* contacts with some of this stuff. Here's how.

There are two types of guidelines here for us to consider and make practical decisions in these areas. First, the Bible teaches certain clear-cut, moral PRECEPTS to follow, some of which are contained in the Ten Commandments, for instance. Lying, cheating, stealing, etc., are wrong for any believer at any time. Also, a believer shouldn't marry a non-believer or swear casual oaths (i.e. "As God lives, I will never…" or "By heaven, I will never…"). There are other fairly clear "do's and don'ts" in the Scriptures, but unfortunately nothing is found like, "Television is evil; don't watch it!"

However, there are also general PRINCIPLES for each of us to apply with *wisdom*. These are not clear-cut commandments binding everyone to practice them without failure, but they're still very important to apply. Here's one…

"Abstain from every form of evil." (I Thessalonians 5:22)

This is a broadly defined guideline, meaning we should avoid and not participate in any "visible form, shape, appearance, outward show or kind of evil."* No specifics are given, but, essentially, we must avoid every form of obvious sinful behavior, even if it's small.

Yes, sincere believers might differ at times as to identifying a specific "form" of sin that they are to avoid. To use the same example above, one person might completely remove the television from his/her home, because it has evil in its programming, while another would eliminate from their viewing only particular programs that are indeed offensive. There's some elbow room, here, and believers must apply wisdom, not legalism. But, the danger comes when one "gives in" and partakes of some behavior in one of two slip-sliding ways.

1. A person indulges in something he or she is unsure about or *believes* is sinful.
2. A person foolishly continues indulging something that Scripture generally says is dangerous, imprudent, and without wisdom.

* The word for "form" in the original Greek, taken from biblehub. com/1_thessalonians/5-22.htm)

In addition, the Bible talks about kindness, love, purity, holiness, etc., which are again conceptual principles and general guidelines to apply to our lives. One Christian may see a more graphic depiction of evil in a movie, for example, and call it "an evil thing and one shouldn't watch it at all." But, another sees the depiction as real, but not necessarily sinful in intent (tempting to himself). Therefore, he says that one should be mature enough to view it.

So, there's again some room for differing applications and, perhaps, differences in personal strengths and weaknesses. Generally, such differences aren't really insurmountable, if one keeps in mind that it is a *sensible* thing for *serious-minded believers* to avoid places, practices and people that realistically could negatively influence them toward evil in attitude and action. People can differ with the amount of freedom they allow for themselves, of course, but remember that God holds them accountable for their choices. Romans 14:5 is a helpful verse in this situation:

> "One person considers one day more sacred than another; another considers every day alike. Each of them should be fully convinced in their own mind."

Here's one additional bit of wisdom which is very helpful in avoiding compromise and keeping a clear conscience. Keep in mind that this is not an absolute, for wisdom doesn't lay down precepts, only principles for those sincerely committed to seriously spirituality.

> *Though a point of wisdom isn't a command to follow,*
> *it doesn't mean that it's just a gentle suggestion.*

It still is something to carefully consider in our day to day confrontations with this increasingly debased culture in which we find ourselves swimming. And, we are responsible and accountable before God to weight its wisdom, when it applies to us. In this regard, here's my bit of wisdom, which sums up our whole topic:

> *Swimming in swamps is dangerous;*
> *avoid it unless absolutely necessary!*

What am I saying? I'm suggesting that we personally should avoid spiritual danger zones where hungry alligators lurk to make a meal out of a naïve passerby. *Unfortunately, compromising believers do not often heed such wisdom*, but instead enjoy making excuses and taking *unnecessary* liberties and spiritual risks. Some are "lucky" and don't get eaten, but some get scarred from having too many close encounters. Wise believers keep a safe distance from evil influences and predators.

So, don't be a monk, sitting on a bed of nails, trying to avoid contact with every possibility of evil...you'll need to drop out of life! On the other hand, don't "monkey around" with predatorially evil behaviors or associations, either. Living out there in the jungle is serious business, and you don't want to become a snack for a ruthless, spiritual carnivore!

"Unguarded closeness to sin or sinners courts compromise, spawns spiritual insensitivity, and corrupts integrity. Reasonable distance, however, develops critical discernment, necessary discipline and enduring spiritual dedication."

Your Spiritual Tool Box

Today's Project:
Stop The Leaks!

Your Blueprint:
"Blessed are those who keep his statutes and seek him with all their heart. They do not compromise with evil, and they walk only in his paths." (Psalm 119:3 NLB)

Keeping It Plumb:

I had to replace some old iron pipes with some copper water pipes in my basement a while ago. After cutting off the old pipe, both ends had to be grooved and wrapped in a putty like substance. Next, I inserted a nut on each side and tightened them. However, one side of the pipe just couldn't be tightened enough, for a small leak continually escaped from the joint. The pressure just kept squirting out water, until I added more putty to that grooved joint and reconnected it.

Similarly, as the pressures of life try forcing us to compromise our values, our integrity can drip away. God wants our spiritual integrity contained and always ready to be used in whatever tasks he has for us. Let's plug up our "spiritual drips," okay!

Golf and Grace

The other day I woke up at 6:15, looked outside and said to myself, "Okay, sun is shining, it's a cloudless and windless day...hey, this is a great morning for a quick 9 holes of golf! I'll be back at 9 am...no problem...then I can start my day." Fantastic idea! So, I jumped out of bed, eager to get started.

"Where are you going?" asked my wife, Kathy.

"The weather's great...gonna go for a quick nine," I responded.

"It's 6 am...you've got to be kidding!" My wife was not impressed with my golf aspirations.

"Nope...need the exercise," I commented, as I pulled some socks out of the drawer. In about 30 minutes, I was on the first tee and driving a ball down the early morning, dew-covered fairway.

Walking down the fairway after the first drive, I asked the Lord to give me some things to share in this chapter of the book. Golf has always had some practical similarities with the Christian life, so here are some spiritual applications from my morning on the links.

Lesson #1: "Nailed It!"

That first drive down the fairway was unusually good. Sometimes in the early morning one's back and shoulders can be a bit stiff. But, this morning my drive went a straight 250 down the center...wow!

I find that life has an abundance of good days for believers. Yes, I know this is America and that not everyone in the world gets up to play, or has good health, for instance. Nevertheless, Scripture is clear that the godly will be blessed, even though that's affected by how we're living our life, by our geographic locality, by our inherited health, etc. I believe that God is not limited by these things, though he allows them to have an influence our lives. In any circumstance that you find yourself, know that God loves you and is in control over every aspect and situation in your life. He can bless you in the midst of less-than-excellent life circumstances or in seemingly perfect situations. Either way, life is always impacted by God's loving sovereignty to some degree.

Lesson #2: On the beach!

Yeah, that's right, I put my 2nd shot in the sand to the right of the green. I just couldn't believe it...after a great, first tee-shot, too.

"Here goes my par," I grumbled. And, sure enough, my sand shot (in kind of heavy, water-soaked sand) did go too far past the cup, so 2 putted for a bogey 5.

Well, life is like that, some good starts and some bad ones, even for believers. Jesus warned us that we will have a degree of "tribulation" in life, so we shouldn't be shocked by it. Of course, difficulties (e.g. simple sand bunkers) are frequently spread around as we go about our daily business, but we ought to accept them, first, and then learn how to best deal with them.

Are you learning how to face simple life stresses, discouragements and push-backs? A lot of the things in this book will help for sure, but for now I would suggest two *fundamental* things: Know both basic Biblical Doctrine (which we'll address in this book) as well as practical wisdom for spiritual living. Doctrines have to do with things like justification, reconciliation, Christology, etc. But, there are practical things, too, which are essential for us to grow spiritually. In golf, these are basic things in your swing, in your stance and in your club choices that make a critical difference in your ultimate success. Similarly, mastering the basics in Christian living...controlling one's mind, maintaining purity, seeking consistent fellowship, praying regularly...all these and more are needed to form a solid spiritual "swing" for a successful life score. Both the doctrinal and the practical are essential.

Lesson #3: Mercy!

It was the fourth hole, a long and difficult par four. Driving from a highly elevated tee, I put the ball just over the 20' wide stream, which ran left to right about 220 yards down the fairway. My second shot had to go another 200 yards or so to an elevated green with woods on the right, a fence in back, and a wide sand trap in front. The best shot was to hit a 3-wood and drop it just to the right of the green. Unfortunately, my shot went to the left, and landed in the sand trap.

"Nuts...how did I do that? Must have been the wind," I thought to myself (a common but inaccurate reason most of the time!). So, I trudged up the long slope to the green and found that my ball had bounced *out* of the water-hardened sand and onto the green about 20 feet from the cup. Unbelievable!

> *"The LORD is gracious and merciful, slow to anger and abounding in steadfast love."* (Psalm 145:8)

God's merciful blessings in our lives are so abundant, we really don't realize the extent of it all. When we get to heaven, it will be fun, God permitting, if we re-run our life disc back to all the times God protected us from loss, kept us from evil and gave us another change to shape up. That's *also* a good thing to remember when dealing with the sins of others *toward us*. Matthew 18:21, 22 says:

> *"Then Peter came to Jesus and asked, "Lord, how many times shall I forgive my brother or sister who sins against me? Up to seven times?"*
> *Jesus answered, "I tell you, not seven times, but seventy-seven times."*

Mercy is a wonderful thing, and all of us need it, because of our tendency to give in to temptation and disobey God. A good golfer learns to forgive himself for a bad shot, otherwise, he'll carry that negativity throughout his game and ruin his score. A healthy believer has learned the value of forgiving others and himself in Christ, when sin pops up here and there throughout the week.

Lesson #4: Surprised By Grace!

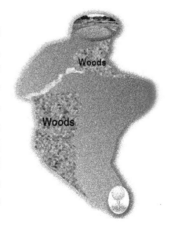

I was up high on the 8th tee, looking over a wide fairway with woods to the left...thick, unforgiving, and impenetrable woods all the way down the left side about 250 yards. The smart play is to drive it at least 50 yards to the right into a wide-open fairway a football field in width. As you can see in the diagram, the fairway curves left around those woods after 250 yards, crosses a stream and then climbs up a hill, on top of which rested the elevated green. It was a par 5 that would challenge Tiger Woods!

Well, I drove the ball solid and long...but, unfortunately to the left! I didn't just pull it into the woods slightly or roll into just the edge of the woods. No, I hit that ball high and long into the very center of it all!

With my usual golf negativity, I remarked to myself, "Okay...there goes my game." As normal for such a wayward shot, I took a 2nd provisional drive just in case I couldn't find the ball (which seemed totally impossible to find, anyway!). You guessed it...I hit that 2nd ball in the same identical spot...deep into the woods.

"This is ridiculous!" I mumbled. So, I grabbed my golf bag, returned my club and stormed off and down the hill along the woods. I knew in my mind that either of those balls were at least 30 feet into thick woods and couldn't possibly have bounced through...*but, I was wrong.* Arriving about 230 yards down the fairway, there were the two balls, laying just 6 feet apart and resting about 10 feet from the edge of the woods...in the fairway. *I simply couldn't believe it!*

"No way!" I shouted out, though no one was around to hear me. How could two balls, hit into thick woods, have ricocheted off a forest of trees perfectly enough to bounce through it all and land right next to each other in the fairway? God was gracious to me beyond imagination!

Grace is like that in life, beyond a simple game of golf, of course. It shocks you into the conscious joy of realizing that God's love is unstoppable and undeterrable. What we think is too bad and too impossible to change, God pulls out his own spiritual club and lays up an iron shot of grace. Instead of bogies, he can pull off unbelievable birdies in our spiritual lives, if we're willing to seriously pursue him and his will for our lives...he's just awesome!

Lesson #5: People Issues

From the 4th hole on, I noticed that there was a two-some moving up from behind. Normally, golf etiquette demands that two people playing the fairway behind you wait until those up ahead are a safe distance away before hitting their balls. However, this two-some seemed very impatient, and continually hit their balls much too close to me for several holes. Now, I was a single player, shooting near par, and moving fast, so I don't know why they were doing this. Perhaps they didn't know or care about the rules. Either way, I stopped and turned around on the 8th hole green, after one of their balls landed 10 feet away, and waved at them to be more careful.

Well, that didn't stop them. So, at the 9th green, after sinking the putt for a par, I crossed over to the club house and asked the manager to "say a few words" to the annoying two-some as they left the 9th shortly thereafter. The one guy started cursing at me and the manager with a host of loud and hateful adjectives. Bottom line? He wanted nothing to do with saying he was sorry or unaware of the rules. It was not an enjoyable scene or a nice ending to an otherwise great game of golf.

Application? Well, as believers, we will always live in a world given to sin. Nasty words, hateful diatribes, dysfunctional relationships, and abusive people will always be around us (and, unfortunately at times, we can be like that, too). In this case, I didn't respond in kind or fight back, I just let the proper authorities try to convince that guy of the danger and inappropriateness of his actions. I believed the manager asked him to play somewhere else next time, and I've not seen him since. Jesus said, *"If it is possible, as far as it depends on you, live at peace with everyone."* For believers, such choices are just *par* for the course.

Your Spiritual Tool Box

Today's Project:
Success

Your Blueprint:
"Be strong and very courageous. Be careful to obey all the law my servant Moses gave you; do not turn from it to the right or to the left, that you may be successful wherever you go. Keep this Book of the Law always on your lips; meditate on it day and night, so that you may be careful to do everything written in it. Then you will be prosperous and successful. Have I not commanded you? Be strong and courageous. Do not be afraid; do not be discouraged, for the LORD your God will be with you wherever you go." (Joshua 1:7-9)

Keeping It Plumb:
Success and failure go together…it's called life…and learning is a critical part of the process (golf seems to have more than its share of learning in it, based upon my usual unimpressive scores). But, keep going and maintain a rigorous commitment to the things of God, and the Lord will be with you in your failures and your successes. The words of Moses to Joshua above have always been an encouragement to me, I hope they are to you as well.

Is Your Worship Genuine?

As moral creatures with consciences, we are involved daily with choices about right and wrong. Even skeptics have to acknowledge this side of us, the side that contemplates moral responsibility for our attitudes, behaviors and choices. Animals and flowers could care less about moral decisions and actions, but human beings have this capacity and use it all the time. This innate recognition of God's existence and relationship within us moves most people to worship.

You've heard of the "atheist in the foxhole" idea, where someone facing immanent death on the battlefield will quickly forget his disgruntled misgivings about the existence of God...and pray for help? It may not be deeply "worshipful," but it's still a fundamental recognition that God is there to call upon in the midst of possible death. When the pressure is on, people know God exists.

However, defining worship in general can be somewhat difficult, depending upon where one has been raised and what type of religious background he or she comes from. So, let's refer to worship as the Bible does, an act of belief in God and of giving him praise for who he is. The old English term of "worth-ship" says it well, I think, for the value or worth we place upon God is shown by the way we live in regard to his commands. If I have great regard for him and see great worth in obeying him, then I will show it by offering praise for who he is. If I have little regard for him and his commandments, then I will not relate to him very much or praise him in the presence of others. So, the *fundamentals* of worship are twofold:

1. Having the *right perspective*
2. Offering *appropriate praise*

Perspective

As I said before, my wife and I enjoy going down to Orlando each year and staying a week at Walt Disney World. Sometimes we stay "on Disney" (at Disney owned hotels) and sometimes we stay "off Disney" (other hotel groups, e.g. Hilton, Marriott, etc.). But, all hotels are very much interested in consumer reports after a stay, asking that we evaluate them on the basis of meeting expectations for cleanliness, service, etc. A good hotel will normally get at least a 3 out of 5-star rating, but the Disney hotels usually score around 4 stars. Hotel occupancy and reservations are greatly affected by these scores, for they communicate how much people value or assign worth to a particular hotel chain. When you read the short descriptions of why people scored them the way they did, all kinds of things pop up, like this real negative evaluation I got off the internet.

> "First of all. the room smelled like someone had been smoking in it continuously. The floor and carpets were disgusting and dirty. No locks to keep outside people away. The hallways smelled the same as my room. To top off this disgusting stay, they double charged me for 4 nights. I'm still awaiting a refund...So, I say to you, be warned." (not a Disney hotel, by the way)

Perspective certainly fuels a person's evaluation of worth! With God, who is always perfect in love and justice, praise flows from our lips to honor him for his blessings toward us. Worship in essence, therefore, is *a mental evaluation or perspective of who God is*...perfectly kind, loving, gracious, merciful, just, righteous, holy and so many other wonderful attributes. This perspective part of worship quietly resonates upon our understanding of the innate goodness of Almighty God. It needs no outward demonstrations or expressions, for it is an acknowledgement of the profound worth he is to us as we reflect upon his nature.

Praise

However, we also enjoy *expressing* what we understand and feel about God in words, attitudes, music, art, writings, drama, etc. Our inner faith and understanding about the Lord may move us to express this sense of worth outwardly with emotion and creativity. In this context, great composers like Bach and Beethoven have composed classical works giving glory to God, and musicians from Asaph to Crosby have praised God magnificently in musical presentations, hymns, cantatas, concerts and choirs. And, in the simple context of the Sunday worship service, groups of believers gather together to hear the Word of God taught and to respond with songs of praise for Christ's mercy and grace in their lives.

It is in this context that some fundamental truths about worship might be helpful for all of us to remember. *First, please understand that worship is an attitude of the heart, not an activity of the body!* Raising one's hands, saying "Amen," shouting "halleluiah," standing up or staying seated, groaning, nodding the head in approval, clapping one's hands…all of these expressions are *personal options and choices*, and are *not demanded by God's Spirit.* He certainly *inspires* within us the heart-praise God deserves, but people *express this* in ways that they individually find comfortable. There is no biblical rule or spiritual norm for outward worship that one is forced to follow by God's Spirit. It is personality and comfort level issues that most often governs how we outwardly express our love for God. Always keep in mind, therefore, that we should practice wisdom in the way we worship, choosing *what is best,* not what is just *personally satisfying.*

So, be careful not to fall into a form of corporate worship at church that is sheer emotionalism or self-generated performance stuff. It happens, believe me, not only is it employed by television evangelists, but by leaders who manipulate worship services for feeling sake, instead for glorifying God. None of that is worship, for *true worship glorifies the message, not the messenger.* Paul says clearly that participants in worship should exercise self-control, which would of necessity include prophets, musicians, teachers and all contributors. *Truth that is profoundly understood and acknowledged, instead of just "felt," is the only truth that significantly transforms a life.*

> "What then shall we say, brothers and sisters? When you come together, each of you has a hymn, or a word of instruction, a revelation, a tongue or an interpretation. Everything must be done so that the church may be built up." (I Cor. 14:26) **Note:** built up means edified, not emotionalized)

"The spirits of prophets are subject to the control of prophets. For God is not a God of disorder but of peace—as in all the congregations of the Lord's people… everything should be done in a fitting and orderly way." (I Cor. 14: 32-33, 40)
Note: disorder and emotionalism doesn't produce profound comprehension, enduring conviction or sustained spiritual growth. Worship or praise may <u>feel</u> good at times, but any inherent feeling is a part of us, not mandated by God.

In addition, always keep in mind that fellowship is for believers, not for unbelievers. We are certainly excited if a non-believer enters the church building to seek and know God. But, too many churches today see the church as an evangelistic tent and a place to gather unbelievers by slowly blending them into its services  or activities, hoping they will eventually come to Christ. This has resulted in a strange mixture of spirituality and carnality coexisting together within the church walls. Sermons become shallow and worship becomes entertainment-driven in order to keep the pews full and the television audience tuned in. In addition, into the church also comes loosening standards in personal attire, entertainment, worship, music, and moral choices, even possible spurious doctrine. Inevitably, discipleship takes a back door to evangelistic numbers and size, stunting spiritual growth and depth among believers. Before long, even worship itself has disintegrated into a *party* atmosphere, full of percussion-pounding music with "touchy-feely" words, "smoke and mirror" presentations, and soft-served sermons. This is not good, and it is a significant problem that's not going to go away very easily.

Remember, the church body is *fundamentally* a "gathering of believers," those who have genuinely embraced the cross of Jesus Christ in their lives. Such a church is deep into teaching about the *cost* of discipleship, spiritual *integrity*, personal *holiness* and enjoys appropriate forms of worship focusing upon gaining *wisdom* instead of waves of emotion. From this type of worship comes a more stable love for God, one that models Christlikeness with spiritual depth and lasting integrity.

Your Spiritual Tool Box

Today's Project:
Giving True Worth To God

Your Blueprint:
"Yet a time is coming and has now come when the true worshipers will worship the Father in the Spirit and in truth, for they are the kind of worshipers the Father seeks."
(John 4:2)
"Do not be yoked together with unbelievers. For what do righteousness and wickedness have in common? Or what fellowship can light have with darkness?" (II Cor. 6:14)

Keeping It Plumb:
Worship is not rigid obedience to a set of rules, but it is also not a free-for-all exercise in emotional excess. Both emotion and structure are necessary and complement each other, but always in their proper place and with appropriate measure. Too much salt in the stew ruins it, right?

So, in the area of worship, remember that we first must worship the Father "in the Spirit," meaning that we must be born again believers. Then, we must let our understanding of truth be our goal, exercising self-control and regarding our feelings. Even in worship we must use wisdom. History is full of wild and crazy behaviors that "believers" have employed to satiate their own desires at the expense of what is genuine, sensible, and Scripturally sound.

Lastly, keep your fellowship times pure, honest and spiritually productive by focusing upon discipleship teaching and commitment concerns. At the same time, continue to reach out enthusiastically to unbelievers both personally and through creative ministry events.

"And let us consider how we may spur one another on toward love and good deeds, not giving up meeting together, as some are in the habit of doing, but encouraging one another—and all the more as you see the Day approaching." (Hebrews 10:24-25)

Failure Happens

A pastor recently made a statement that some didn't like from the pulpit. He said, "God's plan for our lives is full of failure." In support of it, he used Joseph, David and other Biblical examples, but both my wife and I disagreed strongly. We knew what he was trying to say, that believers fall into sin, so don't be unduly guilty or shocked by it. When we fall, we should just get up, confess things, and get back into the race.

But, let's also understand that God doesn't *want us* to fail, nor is he in the business of designing things to trip us up, either. He wants us to learn and grow from our failure, and as little of failure as possible, I might add.

Did you hear about the mother who tried to hide from a salesman? She was relaxing in the tub, when a knock came on the door. Her eight-year old son opened the door to a traveling Bible salesman.

"Hi, son, is your mother home? I'd like to talk with her about God's Truth."

"Hold on, sir," returned the little guy and closed the door. He went upstairs to tell his mother who was there.

"No, Joey, truth is, I don't what to talk with him right now. Tell him I'm not home." Joey then ran downstairs and opened the front door again. The salesman was still there, waiting.

"Mom's in the tub, but she told me to tell you that she's not at home."

Unfortunately, we often try to hide from our failures and sins, keeping such things to ourselves. Though we're *not* told to share every piece of "dirty laundry" with everyone everywhere, confessing our sins and failures is a good thing to do in the presence of a good friend, a pastor, or a trusted family member, for instance. Such humility builds strength of character and finds a place, perhaps, for needed forgiveness and restoration. In James 5:16, God says the following:

> *"Therefore, confess your sins to each other and pray for each other so that you may be healed."*

So, generally speaking, let's always be willing to seek help and healing from a brother or sister in Christ that we trust. All of us fail. To deny or hide it just doesn't make spiritual sense. Be selective, but open up and seek help.

LISTEN

Listening is an art, and requires one to not just open up the ears, but the mind as well. It demands that we are intensively focused and seeking God's guidance, particularly in this area of failure and sin. Sincerely repentant believers search for knowledge and wisdom to handle whatever issue is confronting them. When it's all said and done, we want to get the message *God* is trying tell us.

We should be responsible to listen to the spiritual counsel given through many sources...friends, Pastors, Christian music, Scripture and experience. But, again, I would say that the most important source around which one bases their ultimate decision should be Scripture. Why? Because we know that it contains the absolute Word of God, without error and given specifically to guide us through our lives this side of heaven.

Also, be sure to "search" the Scriptures carefully and prayerfully, in order to *understand* the message in it. We've also got to be sure that we apply it without *"magic,"* too. By that, I mean that not every statement, teaching or promise is specifically meant for us (try to avoid finger pointing for answers!). Each book of the Bible was written in general for all believers to use as common guidelines for spiritual learning. Take the verse in Mark 11:24, for instance:

> *"Therefore, I tell you, all things whatever you pray and ask for, believe that you have received them, and you shall have them..."*

This verse is not a pre-paid *gift-card* for every believer! It is not suggesting that every prayer we pray is going to be granted as long as we show continued faith in receiving it. No, this verse is to be applied to other verses that should also be considered, like this one:

"When you ask, you do not receive, because you ask with wrong motives, that you may spend what you get on your pleasures." (James 4:3)

So, we need faith, but we also need purity and integrity in our lives (among other things as well) in order for God to bless us with answers to our prayers. *Listening intently* to what God might be saying to us is fundamental spirituality.

LEARN

Secondly, there's a big difference between hearing and listening. Intentional listening from the heart is what is needed, and, if done genuinely, it will bring about a *challenge to change.* In other words, we've *learned* some truth or principle from God, which prompts us to *wholeheartedly receive it.* Remember, the context here is about listening to a wide variety of Biblical counsel on how to overcome sin and repetitive failure. Eventually, then, when we deeply understand what God's trying to tell us about our failure or sin, we will experience an "unction" from the Spirit. That's really where listening turns into learning, because learning means *acknowledging* God's truth and then *accepting it.*

Unction is mostly an older term, which essentially means being "smeared" or "anointed" (a Hebrew activity involved in sacrificial worship). The Christian's *first* experience of this is when we felt the Spirit *calling* and *prodding* us deep within in order to reach out to receive Christ as Savior and Lord. Sensing this Gospel prompting and choosing to be receptive to it, we entered into saving faith. In response, he entered our soul to dwell forever, and we were anointed with God's Spirit, pouring over us his abundant mercy and grace.

Similarly, we must *still* be receptive to the Spirit's prodding in our general walk with Christ. Being *sensitive* to God's prompting is key to overcoming sin and failure. You'll recognize God's prompting as an inner, though most likely, inaudible voice, calling you to holiness and purity. God's truth has begun to change you inside, recognizing the need to seriously repent and change your ways. So, listening to a good sermon or hearing some great worship music is good. But, learning from God ultimately means *accepting* God's Word into our hearts.

LAY OUT A PLAN

Finally, the Spirit enlightens our minds and hearts in order to <u>adopt</u> his inner "promptings" and <u>apply</u> them faithfully. The final part of dealing with failure, then, is to *act upon* what God is "challenging you to change." It is not being obsessed with guilt and remorse, or hiding away and "licking your wounds" for 6 months! Humble yourself, confess your sin (regardless of your feelings), and restore your relationship with God through times of intimate prayer, Scriptural study and meaningful fellowship. Also, take the time to seek the counsel of key believers in your life for insight and encouragement.

Lasting spiritual growth appears when we begin to seriously adopt and apply what God is telling us. It may mean changing your schedule each day to deepen your devotional life, or it might mean removing some unwise relationships. It could mean purifying your mind or eliminating some compromising influences in your television watching or internet surfing. Whatever, carve out the necessary time slots and add the critical disciplines God is asking you to do invest in your spiritual future. Remember, sin is like a bad tooth...it just doesn't want to be removed easily or without pain. So, step up to the pump, friend, for God is not as impressed by the spiritual truths you learn, *but by the spiritual truths you apply!*

Your Spiritual Tool Box

Today's Project:
Go Forward, Not Backwards

Your Blueprint:
"Not that I have already obtained all this, or have already arrived at my goal, but I press on to take hold of that for which Christ Jesus took hold of me. Brothers and sisters, I do not consider myself yet to have taken hold of it. But one thing I do: Forgetting what is behind and straining toward what is ahead, I press on toward the goal to win the prize for which God has called me heavenward in Christ Jesus."
(Phil. 3:12-14)

Keeping It Plumb:

"We didn't lose the game,

we just ran out of time!"
A word of encouragement from Vince Lombardi

"Your Attitude Determines Your Altitude"
A positive and instructive insight from Zig Ziglar.

Demons and Demigods

I came across the picture above and immediately inserted it into this chapter. It clearly describes the efforts of our unseen enemy, Satan, and his hosts of insidious, corrupted and fallen spirits we call demons. There is an entire, hidden world all around us existing with the singular intent of causing havoc and destruction to God's creation. This is the clear and fundamental message in the Bible that shouldn't be ignored. We see the influence of evil spirits in demagogues like Hitler, in the insidious philosophy of political correctness, in the evil morality often portrayed in entertainment, in the decisions and policies of vacillating political leaders, and in the liberal bastions of our modern educational institutions.

In addition, there are many false religions and cultic groups out there that have a host of gods and godlike characters in their worship or teaching. The Greek Pantheon was a good example of this, hosting multitudes of gods and god-like heroes, most beset by foibles and character flaws, which is probably why they were so popular among the common folk. The Shintoism religion literally teaches that millions of godlike spirits are floating around in people, birds, animals, and in all parts of creation. Indeed, fallen mankind has followed his imagination and has devised all kinds of spiritual fantasies and false teaching. In addition, there are countless other cultic groups propagating spiritism, devil worship, and other demonic focused or sensually focused forms of worship. Paul addresses this in Romans chapter 1:21-25.

"For although they knew God, they neither glorified him as God nor gave thanks to him, but their thinking became futile and their foolish hearts were darkened. Although they claimed to be wise, they became fools and exchanged the glory of the immortal God for images made to look like a mortal human being and birds and animals and reptiles. Therefore, God gave them over in the sinful desires of their hearts to sexual impurity for the degrading of their bodies with one another. They exchanged the truth about God for a lie, and worshiped and served created things rather than the Creator—who is forever praised. Amen"

Although mankind continues to toy with evil spirits and fantasies about these things, God has sent his son into the World to inform it of its corrupted way of thinking and worshiping. Jesus came into the world to bring us the Truth about life, as well as a way to be saved from demon-rooted hopelessness, sin and spiritual death. By faith in Christ as Savior and Lord, we can be set free from the shackles of demonic influence and experience the joy of spiritual wholeness and eternal life. As the picture above suggests, demons are fallen spirits, ruled by Satan and expressly committed to reaching up to mankind and pulling him down to death and destruction, both personally, culturally and nationally. Yet, God's Truth is revealed by Christ Jesus and in the Scriptures, being the only solution for evil and the singular hope for fallen mankind.

There are three basic things we need to know about facing demonic influence in our own lives. First, it is **real** and **insidious**. By way of example, my wife and I do enjoy Disney vacations, but I'm also aware that the company has, to a degree, become a source of moral liberalism. It supports Christian values to a large part, but it also incorporates homosexuality and multi-culturalism, for instance, into its corporate culture. Also, its most recent addition of "Rivers of Light" in the Animal Kingdom, to my mind, has strong Shintoism overtones in its presentation. At present, most of our Disney vacations still seem to be enjoyable and free from an inundation of politically correct nonsense or cultural pressure *directly antagonistic* to Christian values. BUT…there may come a time when this may not be the case, and our consciences may dictate to us a different place to vacation.

My point is that the world is under the influence *everywhere* of demonic forces in its thinking. This doesn't mean we should extract ourselves from every contact with such a company or person so influenced, for as Paul reminds us regarding removing ourselves from non-believers, "we would have to leave the world." Still, recognizing it and avoiding *unnecessary* or *overly influential involvement* with it is wise. Such a decision will vary among believers, of course, but all of us should re-evaluate regularly the entertainment in which we participate.

Secondly, Satan and his demonic following do not exist outside of the control of God and his angels. Scriptures tells us that angels are fighting against evil and Satan, holding him at bay and only allowing them to succeed in accordance with the will of God. Just as a car cannot hit and kill us apart from the providential will of God, neither can these evil entities do anything to us without permission from our heavenly Father (see Job, chapters 1-2).

Thirdly, demonic hosts can oppress and possess human beings. By oppression is meant that they can "come against" believers and/or non-believers at times in order to cause harm or to entice them toward evil. Hence, demons can cause blindness, loss of hearing and many other physical diseases and abnormalities, along with intense mental pressures and suggestive influences (please be advised that not all, perhaps not even most diseases are involved with some sort of demonic influence).

By possession, we mean that non-believers (not believers) can be "over-taken" by these evil spirits and controlled to the point of complete mental derangement, and capable of committing horrific acts of evil. The believer, though at times seriously influenced by such spiritual beings, cannot be owned or fully possessed by them, because believers are indwelt by God's Spirit.

> "…and who has also put his seal on us and given us his Spirit in our hearts as a guarantee…" (II Corinthians 1:22)

Examples of demonic influence include King Saul, who is an Old Testament example of a man once filled with the Spirit. He turned away in disobedience and eventually found himself possessed by a demonic entity, which caused him great physical pain and a relentless, evil passion to kill his young friend, David. In the New Testament, Scripture says that Satan filled the heart of Ananias, causing him to withhold money from the church and then to lie about it (Acts 5:1-11). Also, Peter was "called out" by Christ because of his Satan-influenced thinking:

> *"But he turned and said to Peter, "Get behind me, Satan! You are a hindrance to me. For you are not setting your mind on the things of God, but on the things of man."* (Matthew 16:23)

I've talked with missionaries, who understand that Satan and his demonic forces are more active in the mission fields around the world. We see a TV program about a witch doctor's curse and think nothing of it, but missionaries in such voodoo-infested cultures know that such things can be very real.

People in "un-Christianized" areas around the globe do get involved with demonic forces intentionally and seek their influence, just like the spiritually corrupt nations that oppressed Israel in Old Testament times. In addition, even people in "civilized" cultures like our own, who are deep into drugs, carnal entertainments and sexual pleasures, open up spiritual doors for demonic oppression and/or possession. As someone has said, "Satan isn't behind every bush," but he does hang around a few trees here and there, so be aware and advised.

The Apostle Paul also clearly says that we as believers are in a spiritual war and need to put on God's armor in order to win.

> *"For our struggle is not against flesh and blood, but against the rulers, against the authorities, against the powers of this dark world and against the spiritual forces of evil in the heavenly realms. Therefore, put on the full armor of God, so that when the day of evil comes, you may be able to stand your ground, and after you have done everything, to stand. Stand firm then, with the belt of truth buckled around your waist, with the breastplate of righteousness in place, and with your feet fitted with the readiness that comes from the gospel of peace. In addition to all this, take up the shield of faith, with which you can extinguish all the flaming arrows of the evil one. Take the helmet of salvation and the sword of the Spirit, which is the word of God."* (Ephesians 6:12-13)

<u>How To Recognize and Overcome Demonic Influence</u>

First, you may be asking me, "Okay, but how to I recognize him?" Satan and his demonic hosts live in a world of lies and energetically oppose God's Scriptural Truth. I have a friend in my men's study group, who married a woman practicing Shintoism (before he came to Christ). We pray for her to come to Christ, but we also clearly see the evidences of demonically destructive forces at work in their marriage. Shintoism is steeped in spirit worship, having beings that supposedly manifest themselves everywhere and in everything. My friend has consistently noted spiritually evil compulsions and outbursts in her that seem so "caustic and controlling," that they could rightfully be explained by some degree of demonic forces at work from her involvement with Shintoism since she was a child. In many ways, she's as normal and kind as anyone, but her unusually strong and *animated* rejection of her husband's faith, as well as against anything Christian, speaks to the possibility of such an influence.

Satan is evil to the core and, therefore, produces the results that evil always brings, things like suffering, physical disease, mental issues, as we discussed above. But, of course, this fallen and sinful world can bring on evil results on its own, with no assistance from demons at all. Many, if not most, physical diseases and mental illnesses have roots in heredity, physical disasters and other "natural" causes. Theologically, the Bible refers to all this "natural" stuff as the results of living in the "state of sin," where fallen creation is simply experiencing the results of living apart from intimacy with God.

So, it is not always possible to distinguish from what source evil comes, other than to say that demonic **oppression** is probably fairly common (based upon Ephesians 6). However, demon **possession** is less common and more symptomatic of individuals who have *extreme* agitation or aggression, *superhuman* strength, or behaviors showing a *complete loss of moral control,* usually accompanied by *some involvement* with cults, drugs, porn or other such demonic gateways. We can learn a lot from "Legion," the crazed man that Jesus confronted and healed.

> *"When they came to Jesus, they saw the man who had been possessed by the legion of demons sitting there, clothed and in his right mind; and they were afraid. When they came to Jesus, they saw the man who had been possessed by the legion of demons sitting there, clothed and in his right mind; and they were afraid."* (Mark 15:15)

We can see that before he was healed, he was running around unclothed, cutting himself, out of his mind and unable to be bound. Now, here he is, calm, controlled and at peace with himself and with others…what a miracle…praise God!

Second, in the Ephesians passage above, Paul lists mental *defenses* we must apply, when facing demonic influence. The only one that is *offensive* is the Word of God, which is characterized as a sword. I take this to mean that God's Word is a powerful resource of incredible spiritual influence…greater than anything in the demonic world…and able to pierce and slay the evil thoughts that are attacking us. James even says that if we draw near to God first (and, therefore, to his Word, which is implied), then Satan will flee from us.

> *"So, give yourselves to God. Stand against the devil, and he will run away from you."* (James 4:7)

Peter says that the when we resist Satan by faith in the midst of all our struggles and sufferings, Satan will eventually succumb to the Spirit's power, and we will instead become stronger.

> *"Be alert and of sober mind. Your enemy the devil prowls around like a roaring lion looking for someone to devour. Resist him, standing firm in*

the faith, because you know that the family of believers throughout the world is undergoing the same kind of sufferings. And the God of all grace, who called you to his eternal glory in Christ, after you have suffered a little while, will himself restore you and make you strong, firm and steadfast." (I Peter 5:8-10)

Please understand that demonic influence is real and prevalent in various ways and in various contexts. Wear your spiritual armor confidently, be cognizant of his ways, and focus your faith upon Jesus and his Word. Satan cannot overcome these things, for God's Spirit is stronger and enables us to win.

Lastly, be wise…don't toy with evil attitudes or behaviors in any compromising context! God's power is absolutely able to overcome anything Satan is capable of doing, for he is a simple created being gone bad. However, opening up to his influence by unwise involvement with cultic, carnal and/ or spirit-focused participation, can be a highway for him to travel in your direction. *Make sure the light is RED!*

Your Spiritual Tool Box

Today's Project:
God's Power Exceeds All Others

Your Blueprint:

"…even if our gospel is veiled, it is veiled to those who are perishing. The god of this age has blinded the minds of unbelievers, so that they cannot see the light of the gospel that displays the glory of Christ, who is the image of God." (II Cor. 4:2,4)

Keeping It Plumb:

Fundamental victory over demonic influence is found by staying focused upon Truth. It's not the result of listening to the lies or fantasies Satan whispers into our minds or the evil rantings he shouts at us from the non-believing world around us. In the long run, spiritual maturity will hinge upon our ability to discern, hold onto and focus upon the many strategic truths found in God's Word.

"The seductive whispers of Satan can be overwhelming unless overpowered by deeply embedding God's Word in our hearts."

Facing Your Goliath!

You've probably read about David's amazing defeat of Goliath the Philistine. He was about 10 feet tall and probably weighed over 600 lbs. In the morning, he would step out in front of his battle line and approach King Saul's men, shouting obscenities and all kinds of demeaning things. He could pick up any one of us with one hand and pummel us into submission or simply slice a person in two.

Most often, the spiritual battles we face are not against physical things like relationships, professional struggles and/or financial hardship. Usually, our struggles deal with what's going on inside of us, like unrelenting lust, pride, jealousy, anger, fear, hate, prejudice, etc. Make no mistake about it, however, these foes are not patsies or pushovers. They can be vicious antagonists, which can disable us from becoming mature believers and trusted servants.

We've already talked about some of this, when we looked at overcoming habits. But, there are some perspectives that can really help us when facing critical issues, repetitive sins and those same giants that seem to keep tripping us up. The first *fundamental* strategy is to know your enemy.

KNOW YOUR ENEMY

Loud and abusive giants are quite common in our spiritual travels. They come in the form of *inner compulsions that can be represented in the following ways:*

"My name is **O. U. R. Uppity.** I won't settle for being anything less than the center of attraction. No one is more deserving of the loud praises and tumultuous accolades I treasure. I love it when people talk about how good I look and how much I accomplish. It's too bad everyone can't be as wonderful as I am."

My mission? I corrupt genuine ministry and stifle true spiritual growth, for it's all about me. I resist the Spirit, serve self-interests, and bring disruptive issues to people and programs, when I am allowed to function freely.

"My name is **Lascivious I. Lust.** I'm a bit schizophrenic because sometimes I like to come on with overwhelming power, but at other times my personality is quite sly, secretive and sinister. Either way I enjoy the game of enticing human beings to satisfy their desires with outrageous displays of uncontrolled sensuality. My middle name is "I" for indulgence, for I work inside with Pernicious Avarice, my cousin, to enflame all kinds of sinful desires against the will of God.

My mission? I erode consistency and integrity, while breaking families apart. I enjoy enslaving humans with captivating chains of demonic desire. I mess up their lives with shame and guilt, while sidelining them from significant service for their Master.

"My name is **Antonio Angerfit.** I love to emotionally explode over things in relationships and "say it as it is," without worrying about how I say it. I have no patience for idiots, I hate people who try to control me, and I will never be put down by anybody. If anybody wants to fight about it...well, I'm ready, I can tell you that!"

My mission? I react angrily when impatient and in disagreement with others, destroying harmony and fellowship with self-focused disruption. I particularly love being enabled to do my thing without interference from others, who just sit by and tolerate my outbursts of crude emotion.

"My name is **I. M. Dubious.** I give my clients an obsessive need for knowledge and a hopeless quest for certainty. I stir people's minds and push their strained emotions to the point of exhaustion as I get them to question everything down to the tiniest bit of knowledge, especially as it pertains to God.

<u>My mission</u>? Finite and limited human thinking is my battle zone, unanswered questions my weapons and doubt my target. I disrupt personal peace, disengage functional life skills, and destroy productive ministry.

Perhaps you recognize those well-known giants above. Even apart from the influence of such oppressive giants, the fact is that all of us are a bunch raucous rebels in the inner recesses of our sinful hearts. Every so often our fallen natures expose the depth of our depravity, and we do things that describe us in the following ways:

> ### Some Everyday Goliaths
> ...A proud, manipulative and self-seeking egotist.
> ...A carnal, indulgent and self-satisfying fool.
> ...A bitter, judgmental and self-appointed critic.
> ...A jealous, resentful and self-pitying complainer
> ...A lazy, procrastinating and self-excusing bum.
> ...An angry, demanding and self-willed demagogue.
> ...A compassionless and self-justifying antagonist.

Can you relate? I can, even though none of us like to face the truth about ourselves, for rarely do we confess the deepest issues residing in our hearts. Nevertheless, we possess a giant-infested spiritual geography for nasty Goliaths to roam and take control. So, how do we handle these loud and rebellious antagonists? Here's a short list of solutions.

Like David, **get offended by evil!** David was personally offended by the disrespect and devaluation of Jehovah that Goliath was shouting out. His close walk with God made him very sensitive to this stuff and impelled him to act. As believers grow older in the faith, sadly, they tend to become more "casual" toward sin, when they should become more sensitive to it and cognizant of it instead. On the national front, liberalism is quickly deteriorating cultural sensitivity to traditional, Biblical and American values in this country. When President Obama allowed homosexual marriages, stood up for street violence in political protesting, and created governmental socialism in the Affordable Health Care Act, I believe the clock was set for the complete disintegration of our country in the near future. The tide cannot be turned back unless a significant moral revival is begun at the hand of God.

Like David, **step up and challenge sinful behaviors.** David couldn't stand Goliath's rebellious rhetoric and had to respond appropriately. He spoke up for the truth and boldly shared it with the king. So, speak up in your classrooms, in your school system, in your work environment, and in your church meetings for what is pure and wholesome. In your personal life, avoid just co-existing with Satan's taunts and compromising supporters. Step out in kindness and boldness for godly attitudes and behaviors no matter where you are.

Like David, **take on giants by faith, not in your own strength.** David could have put on Saul's armor and been defensively protected. But, he never would have been able to freely swing a sling and topple a taunting Goliath. He offered himself completely to God and his will, and God answered his trust.

Whatever the style or size of your giant, remember that our weaponry is not of this world.

> *"For though we live in the world, we do not wage war as the world does. The weapons we fight with are not the weapons of the world. On the contrary, they have divine power to demolish strongholds. We demolish arguments and every pretension that sets itself up against the knowledge of God, and we take captive every thought to make it obedient to Christ."*
> (II Corinthians 10:3-5)

Like David, **give the glory to God, not yourself.** David also could have sung a psalm to the ingenuity and inventiveness of his own weapon and how it brought down an overpowering enemy. Instead, he refused the accolades and praised Jehovah, his Lord and the true defender of Israel. What a hero...what a guy!

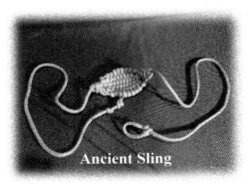
Ancient Sling

Your Spiritual Tool Box

Today's Project:
God's Giant Slayers

Your Blueprint:
"I can do all things through Christ who strengthens me."
(Phil. 4:13)

Keeping It Plumb:

I've not heard of another giant killing event since David accomplished this might feat somewhere around 900AD. Why is that, by the way? The bigger question is, "Why aren't there more miracles around to experience?" Well, as one friend said, "If miracles were more commonplace, we would have to call them regulars!"

My point is that we don't really need a lot of miracles, because God is mostly in the business of rewarding faith and showing our trust in Him. Christianity is not a religious side show. On the other hand, I do think that God would grant us more miraculous works of grace, if believers really wanted and expected them. Too often, I think, we tend to not even ask for one, when trying to deal with a difficulty, a disease or some other sort of painful experience.

I also think we're insensitive to the cold spirituality all around us and the clinging sensuality that lies like a mist on the ground of our world. We should rather be offended by the sin around us and "be a David," sensing and hating evil, calling it out, and then cutting all personal ties with it. This attitude is perhaps what is missing and why God isn't blessing us with more miraculous manifestations.

"Know Yourself"

This concept has been around a long time in philosophy, probably because it carries a lot of truth with it. Many have quoted it, developed it and applied it to our "human condition" since antiquity, including Benjamin Franklin in his *Poor Richard's Almanack*. He observed the following: "There are three things extremely hard - steel, a diamond, and to know one's self." I agree, it is very difficult to learn the truth about who we really are inside, our actual motivations, capabilities, our deepest desires and our worst fears.

The Bible says that all this type of inner "stuff" belongs to the heart, which is the center and innermost part of everything...intellect, inclination and intention. Unfortunately, this inner person, created by God for good, became corrupted with self-centered desires and stubborn self-will, antagonistically set against God. The heart's tendency is to harden itself within its own world, impervious and impenetrable to God's truth and spiritual reality. Here's an example.

You've heard of Murphy's law? An engineer working at Edwards Air Force Base found a technical error made by another worker and said, *"If there's any way to do it wrong, he will find it."* Dr. John Paul Stapp, a project worker, thought the concept was unique and helpful for avoiding technical errors, so he expanded it into a short list of humous sayings. (www.thoughtco.com/murphys-laws-explain-unfathomable-truths-2832861)

Well, I've applied it to golf (you've guessed by now that I really enjoy the game, right?). Here are three of my principles:
- A perfect drive off the tee will always be followed by a lousy fairway shot, which is directly proportional to how good the drive was. A great drive always produces a terrible 2nd fairway hit. My advice is, therefore, to never hit anything better than an average drive off the tee!
- If you hit the ball with an iron to a green bordered by a small and seemingly unnoticeable sand trap, there is an 85% chance you will be on the beach when you walk up to the green…regardless of the size of the sand trap or green. So, always aim for the trap, not the green!
- You can mimic the swing of a Tiger Woods, line up a putt like an Arnold Palmer or dress like a Payne Stewart, but your ball will still slice, hook and worm-burn regularly. However, if you dress like a bum you may do a little better…not much, but at least people will just notice *you* instead of your terrible shot.

I won't belabor the issue, but golf is a hard game to understand and even harder to perform. But, it does offer some interesting challenges easily applied to the Christian life. One such application has been very personal with me, for it has to do with who you think you are. I've always had enough raw talent in golf to be able to pull off some good shots on the links. But, that's where the rub is…I don't seem to be able to do it with professional repeatability, and that's frustrating. To know that you can do it, but you just can't get that perfect par game, is annoying and drives some golfers to throw a club into the air at least once a game.

Now, I'm not a club thrower, but I do get discouraged and negative, when my "Murphy's Golf Laws" seem to be evidencing themselves in my game. What God wanted me to "know about myself" recently was that my overwhelming efforts to become a par golfer revealed a subtle form of pride dwelling deep within me. I thought too much of myself and drove myself to *be* the best, rather than just *do* the best. I believe that God respects those who try to do their best in any task they undertake. But, he doesn't respect those who *always have to be the best*…that's prideful, and it keeps God from using us for his best purposes. But, of course, this is just one person and one example of what we're talking about. Let's look at a short list of other ways we can fall into the trap of not "knowing ourselves."
- Pastor Pete, who hasn't yet acknowledged to himself his wandering eye for the ladies, fails to put a window in his study door for accountability.

- Deaconess Mary Sue enjoys organizing the food for church events, but as of yet won't recognize her over-controlling and dominating nature, as she barks commands at the servers for the summer picnic.
- Bible Study attendee Paul likes to lie in wait at the Men's Study Night at church, so he can drop a pre-loaded, provocative question just at the right time. Everyone jumps in to answer it, and Paul gets his reward - attention.
- Parishioner Paul hired Joe, his friend from his church, to cut the church lawn for him, while he was away on vacation. Joe was to cut the two-acre property and trim all the bushes. When Paul returned, the grass was not done well, having uneven spots all around, and the bushes were cut unevenly. Paul asked him to redo it, so he could pay him, but Joe said no and that he would sue him for the money. Paul showed up in court, but Joe didn't show up. He knew he was wrong, but wasn't willing to face the issue of his own poor workmanship.

This type of thing happens often with in the body of Christ. It seems that believers...all of us...like being forgiven and are quick to make initial changes after repentance. Then, things unfortunately begin to slow up in the process of sanctification, and that inner person with all of its "undiscovered country" isn't really explored too much. Some of the same rough and sinful terrain remains uncharted or at least unchanged. Paul addresses this in Ephesians 4:17-24:

> "So, I tell you this, and insist on it in the Lord, that you must no longer live as the Gentiles do, in the futility of their thinking. They are darkened in their understanding and separated from the life of God because of the ignorance that is in them due to the hardening of their hearts. Having lost all sensitivity, they have given themselves over to sensuality so as to indulge in every kind of impurity, and they are full of greed. That, however, is not the way of life you learned when you heard about Christ and were taught in him in accordance with the truth that is in Jesus. You were taught, with regard to your former way of life, to put off your old self, which is being corrupted by its deceitful desires; to be made new in the attitude of your minds; and to put on the new self, created to be like God in true righteousness and holiness."

The sad thing here is that unbelievers see that we believers haven't changed all that much, and few are willing to make the commitment to Christ that can indeed change their lives. When Jesus said, "You are the light of the world," he meant in part that this is a goal to fulfill, which involves ongoing, intentional change. The question we must ask ourselves is this:

*Are we willing, because of our love for Jesus Christ,
to really look at ourselves deeply enough in order to
make dramatic changes in attitude and behavior,?*

Your Spiritual Tool Box

Today's Project:
Look Into God's Mirror

Your Blueprint:
"Therefore get rid of all moral filth and the evil that is so prevalent and humbly accept the word planted in you, which can save you... Do not merely listen to the word, and so deceive yourselves. Do what it says. Anyone who listens to the word but does not do what it says is like someone who looks at his face in a mirror, and after looking at himself, goes away and immediately forgets what he looks like. But whoever looks intently into the perfect law that gives freedom, and continues in it—not forgetting what they have heard, but doing it—they will be blessed in what they do." (James 1:21-25)

Keeping It Plumb:

Take a few minutes today to take a longer look in God's mirror, the Word of God. Do you see anything that you haven't seen before? Is there something spiritually ugly that needs to be removed by the Divine Surgeon from Calvary?

The Expectation of Blessing

"Why are you a Christian?"

I wonder if that might be one of the qualifying questions the Lord Jesus asks us upon seeing him for the first time at heaven's gate. Yes, the only correct answer is, "I believe in you, Jesus, as my Savior and Lord." But, what if he seeks to test the genuineness of that assertion and asks it a second time.

"Yes, but why are you a Christian?" Jesus probes. "You know, my friend," he continues, "Not everyone who says Savior and Lord is a believer." Such a question at that critical point in time has got to shake you up a bit, even if your faith is genuine. That's because your sincerity is at question, and it cuts deep into your heart commitment. On the other hand, if your response is nothing more than a contrived response anyway, perhaps it reveals the sad realization of hopeless separation and spiritual indebtedness that remains unpaid.

So, since we're on this side of heaven, let's ask the question of ourselves. "Why *am* I a Christian?" It begs a sincere and truthful response, beyond the essential response of belief in Christ. One answer I think the Lord would be pleased with is, "I asked You to be my Savior and Lord at an early age, Jesus, and all of my life I've sincerely sought to obey you and find your blessing in all I do."

The word *blessing* connotes the idea of *beneficial reward from God*. A true believer wants to please the Lord Jesus, because he or she knows that therein lies great blessing (living in favor with God). Again, *true* faith values God's right to rule our lives, and in doing this we know we will enjoy the benefits of having God's grace and mercy working in everything. Peter talks about this in his letter to the churches.

> *"Finally, all of you, be like-minded, be sympathetic, love one another, be compassionate and humble. Do not repay evil with evil or insult with insult. On the contrary, repay evil with blessing, because to this you were called **so that you may inherit a blessing**. For, "Whoever would love life and see good days*** (my emboldened) *must keep their tongue from evil and their lips from deceitful speech. They must turn from evil and do good; they must seek peace and pursue it. **For the eyes of the Lord are on the righteous and his ears are attentive to their prayer, but the face of the Lord is against those who do evil.**"* I Peter 3:8-12

Do you see that the heart of a true believer desires and seeks to do God's will **precisely because he believes in who He is**...Almighty, God, Creator of the universe, and the Holy One who holds the keys to eternal life? As a result, maturing believers have a *fundamental fear* (deep respect) for God's innate right to examine their faith and sound the depth of their spiritual integrity. Knowing this, they also seek his favorable blessings by living a life of obedient faith. If someone doesn't really care about such things, it belays a godless and self-righteous heart.

So, why is the fundamental importance for believers in asking the question, "Why am I a Christian?" It's important because it always prods us forward, and engenders an "expectation of blessing" mindset within us. An obedient faith lifestyle brings *great blessing and joy* into our lives this side of heaven and, therefore, offers **great motivation** for us to persevere in the faith.

My bank was bought out by another bank recently, so all my accounts were transferred to the new bank...same account numbers, just a new bank name. However, along with the change came a gift of 100,000 reward points from the new bank to be used for purchases, dining cards, rental cars, hotels, etc. The total worth was about $200, which paid for a rental car for our trip to Mickey this year!

Because I was a customer in good standing when the transfer came, I had an *"expectation of blessing"* for future use of those reward points. In the same way, when we are spiritually in good standing with Christ Jesus...free from intentional and significant sin...there should be a *great expectation of blessing* in our walk with God. That's the challenge Peter places before us in the above passage.

So, here's some fundamentally good news for us all...**God wants to bless us!** He desires to shower upon us his bountiful riches of mercy and grace in real time. It's ours to look forward to, both in this life and in the next, as long as we are genuine believers in Christ **and** are walking an obedient path in our daily travels at work, at home, in church, etc. I didn't say a "perfect" path, okay. No believer is perfectly obedient in every aspect of his or her life.

"God's favor and blessing is given out, whether sparingly or bountifully, in proportion to our compliance in obeying his will."

But, the challenge is still there...live out your faith in obedience and you can expect God's beneficial blessing in your life. There will, of course, be seasons of difficulty or pain, where God may be refining, chastising or testing us for higher purposes. Overall, however, we have the confidence that God's loving kindness is actively working behind *everything* we experience...he's got our backs! Here's some relevant promises:

General Blessings James 1:25
"The man who looks intently into the perfect law that gives freedom, and continues to do this, not forgetting what he has heard, but doing it – he will be blessed in what he does."

Material Things Matt. 6:31-33
"So, do not worry, saying, 'What shall we eat?' or 'What shall we drink?' Or, 'What shall we wear?' For the pagans run after all these things, and your heavenly Father knows that you need them.
But seek first his kingdom and his righteousness, and all these things will be given to you as well."

Guidance Prov. 3:5, 6
"Trust in the LORD with all your heart and lean not on your own understanding; in all your ways submit to him, and he will make your paths straight."

Wisdom Proverbs 3:13
"Blessed is the man who finds wisdom..."

Generosity Deut. 15:10-11 (NLT)
"Give freely without begrudging it, and the Lord your God will bless you in everything you do..."

One preacher I know says that there is a "premise for every promise." In other words, blessing is to some degree earned by consistently obeying the Word of

God. Every area of living has responsibilities in which we must be faithful to follow God's will, so that God can bless us accordingly.

Your Spiritual Tool Box

Today's Project:

Choose God's Blessing

Your Blueprint:
"And we know that for those who love God all things work together for good, for those who are called according to his purpose."
Romans 8:28

Keeping It Plumb:

The Christian certainly has his/her "ups and downs" like anyone else. We have stresses and difficulties from which we learn more about God and how to please him. But, because of our belief in Christ as Savior and Lord, believers live in a special relationship with God, which the Bible calls his **favor**. Living in God's blessing and favor is a wonderful experience, no matter what stresses or struggles may be included. Jesus is with us and is aware of everything that's going on…no surprises. Here's what living in his favor means:

Forgiveness: Each day is enjoyable, because our guilt over sin has been washed away. Relationship with God is REAL!

Advantage: Each day can is filled with anticipation, because God is working 24/7 to direct and secure our future.

Victory: Each day has impact and influence, because he is within us to accomplish his purposes. He wants us to win and to succeed.

Opportunity: Each day brings ministry, for God has called us to accomplish many things for Him. He will never leave or forsake us.

Reward: Each day is exciting for we are building up a storehouse of rewards in heaven, which we will one day receive from the Lord Jesus.

Are You Willing To Do What You've Never Done To Gain What You've Never Had Or Go Where You've Never Been?

There's A Price To Be Paid

"Suppose one of you wants to build a tower.
*Won't you **first** sit down and estimate **the cost***
to see if you have enough money to complete it?"
Luke 14:28

When I was a boy, my parents built a beautiful, 74' split-level ranch in central Connecticut. They purchased 6 acres of very wooded land with a small rustic cabin in the middle of it. As any ten-year old, I enjoyed playing with the dogs and hiking through the woods, when I wasn't nailing floor boards and building stone walls. At the center of the house was the cabin, which was to eventually become a large living room. But, as it turned out, we couldn't use the cabin walls to save money for the build, because they were just too crooked. This one flaw in my father's original construction plan would cost him thousands of extra dollars, which he hadn't counted on.

Counting the costs of any construction project is a critical component of success, for over-riding and budget-expanding costs create angry clients. One surprising cost-saving budget was for the Empire State Building in New York City, which has a total of 73 elevators, 6,500 windows and 102 floors. The cost without the land was $24,718,000, a cost that would have been twice as much, if it hadn't been built during the Great Depression.

COUNT THE COST

What does it cost one to become a Christian? Well, in the spiritual marketplace there is no cost to the seeker in terms of money. The cost was actually absorbed by Jesus' death upon the cross. So, we do not have to "buy" anything to be saved, become missionaries, or pay for a Christian education. Having said that, the cost to God was significant, and we should "count" it (recognize it, understand it and appreciate it). Jesus, our Creator, loved us so much that he stepped out of heaven's glory to spend three years with a small group of men, teaching them about the kingdom of God and how to be saved. He suffered in place of us that we might not have to die spiritually for all eternity, but have everlasting life. God, therefore, counted the cost to himself even before creation and believed it was worth paying to bring those who trust in Christ to become part his family.

PAY THE PRICE

In another sense, there actually is a price to pay in order to become a Christian. The price to be a Christian is to give over *everything* to him, which is what Lordship and servanthood demands. Even our very lives must be surrendered to God in order to be saved and have eternal life. When looking at it in these terms, many non-believers have found the price to be too high.

> *"For whoever wants to save their life will lose it, but whoever loses their life for me will save it."* Luke 9:24

To be saved from the penalty of our sin, we must recognize this high cost and reckon that it is worth paying in order to find forgiveness. Paying the price in this sense is like finding a diamond in the marketplace that was your parents, who traded it in years before to get cash to pay off hospital bills. Both have died and gone to heaven, but the sentimental value is great. You know it's worth only about $35,000, but the salesperson wants $100,000 in cash by the end of the week for it. So, you sell your home, empty your 401 K and bank accounts, and finally get the money to buy it. You now have little monetarily speaking, but you have the diamond, which is worth much more to you. You've given your all for something beyond dollars and cents, and you're at piece with your decision.

Few believers would argue against the thinking in the above example, as far as it concerns salvation. But, what about our *sanctification?* In other words, are we still willing to pay the ongoing and daily price of living for Christ, which involves self-sacrifice, humility, and self-control instead of materialism, sensuality, and moral license? Sadly, too often we are not willing to pay the price of submission to the will of God in specific areas of challenge. The really sad thing is that the value of godly living and blessing is of far greater worth than anything we try to hold onto. The old saying remains true: *"God cannot pour his abundant grace into hands that are already full."* Paul also said it well:

> *"What is more, **I consider everything a loss** because of the surpassing worth of knowing Christ Jesus my LORD, for whose sake I have lost all things. I consider them garbage, that I may gain Christ."* Phil. 3:8

STAY THE COURSE

Okay, assuming we're willing to count the cost and pay the price for spiritual living and blessing, only one thing remains – "staying the course." That's good, old-fashioned perseverance to the things of Christ.

Someone was upset with everything in life...his job, his wife, his church... everything. He turned to a friend and asked, *"I'm at the end of my rope. What should I do?"*

The friend looked at him compassionately and responded, *"Hang on!"*

Every one of us has times in his or her spiritual life that immerses us in discouragement and self-doubt. We pray for answers, but they don't seem to come. We ask for help, and things don't seem to change. We seek God's strength to overcome our weaknesses, but we seem to sink only further into sin.

The problem in most of this is that we're impatient and think that our timing is better than God's. It is necessary to exhibit trust during those difficult times...even when the trials continue and relief is nowhere in sight.

Sometimes in the morning I awake early and gaze through the cracks in the window blinds just before dawn. Is it going to be a good day...a sunny day...another day of refreshing beauty from the Lord? Or, is it going to rain and blow in a Buffalo cloud cover that we're so often used to up here (in the winter, it brings usually about 100+ inches of lake effect snow every season!).

So, stay the course and wait for God's sunshine...it always comes when God's perfect timing sends it down to us. Keep yourself intensely focused and busy in kingdom work and you'll be happier and blessed because of it.

"Humble yourselves, therefore, under the mighty hand of God so that at the proper time he may exalt you..." I Peter 5:6

Your Spiritual Tool Box

Today's Project:
Keep On Keeping On!

Your Blueprint:
"In your struggle against sin you have not yet resisted to the point of shedding your blood. And have you forgotten the exhortation that addresses you as sons?
My son, do not regard lightly the discipline of the Lord, nor be weary when reproved by him.
For the Lord disciplines the one he loves, and chastises every son whom he receives.'"
(Hebrews 12:4-8)
"Therefore, lift your drooping hands and strengthen your weak knees, and make straight paths for your feet, so that what is lame may not be put out of joint but rather be healed."
(Hebrews 12:13, 14)

Keeping It Plumb:
Sometimes I really dislike starting a task, like repairing the plumbing or re-doing the wallpaper in a bedroom. But, I usually tell myself, "Hey, it's just part of owning your own home...so get to it, Kenerson. You'll enjoy it when it's finished!" And, I usually do.

Getting the most out of life demands staying the course and following through with what expected of us. This is true physically, and it's true spiritually. You only get out what you put in.

"You'll be tomorrow where you were yesterday unless you change today!"

Male and Female

Our wayward and liberal culture seems determined to undermine the identity of Christian marriage and family. There has developed a huge "political correctness" movement that has essentially washed over this country like a flood. Sex education in many cities is now embattled in an ideological war about having things like "my two mommies" and "Dad's special friend" in the test books for elementary students. Masturbation, condom usage, abortion and much more are now being pushed into the receptive minds of these young children. But, it's a war going on everywhere...higher education, entertainment, media and corporate training programs.

As believers, we must remember that the rules and goals of our spiritual races haven't changed one bit in 2000 years. Culture has changed, but not Christ. Families have gone through a lot of historical change in structure and role identification culturally, but not Biblically. Change can be okay, sometimes even necessary or refreshing, as long as it doesn't challenge the foundations upon which Christian morality and family life rests. We need to be verbally and behaviorally committed to Christian values taught in the Scripture.

- Sexual Roles In The Home -

This is also a hot topic today, but again, Scripture is our guide, not culture. I'm speaking here of what it means to be a man, a woman or a child within the family structure. There is a sound authority structure given in the Bible that has been challenged throughout history by secular society, even by some misguided believers. Let's look at it.

First, men are given primary authority in the home. This means that ultimate decision-making authority and responsibility rests with them.

"For the husband is the head* of the wife as Christ is the head of the church, his body, of which he is the Savior. Now as the church submits to Christ, so also wives should submit to their husbands in everything. Husbands, love your wives, just as Christ loved the church and gave himself up for her to make her holy, cleansing her by the washing with water through the word, and to present her to himself as a radiant church without stain or wrinkle or any other blemish, but holy and blameless. (Eph. 5:23-28)

Now, let me apply this carefully! This doesn't imply that a man should not *delegate* responsibilities to his wife, if the wife happens to be better at something, say, keeping finances, for instance. It *also* doesn't say that the husband should make *all* decisions *apart* from the wife. Frankly, if he's smart, he'll most often seek the opinions of his wife (sometimes children) before making a final decision in most areas. This is both a loving thing to do and a sensible one. So, the marital relationship is *not* meant to be a despotic rule on the part of the husband, nor one that gives him "parental" control over his wife. That is not Scriptural.

"You husbands in the same way, live with your wives in an understanding way, as with someone weaker, since she is a woman; and show her honor as a fellow heir of the grace of life, so that your prayers will not be hindered." (I Peter 3:7)

Decision making and loving communication at every level is critical for marital success. The Bible only says that the *responsibility* of authority (decision making) rests ultimately with the husband, and that the wife needs to respect this. His relationship with her must always be *lovingly* kind and gentle...never despotic, domineering or controlling. Her relationship with him must always be *lovingly* respectful, submissive and supportive.

- Roles In The Church -

"I want men everywhere to lift up holy hands in prayer, without anger or disputing...A woman should learn in quietness and full submission. I do not permit a woman to teach or to have authority over a man; she must be silent. For Adam was formed first, then Eve. (I Tim 2:8 - 3:12)

*The Greek word for "head" is a military term, implying rank or authority.

> *"Subordination, dependence, and difference of nature are the three reasons the early church assigned for the non-participation of women in public vocal ministry, and this regulation of silence was not grounded in...temporary conditions...but was related to a far more basic and fundamental reason, that is, the difference in position and nature of male and female. These are the facts whether we like them or not...which makes all the texts consistent with one another. Whether this agrees with present-day practice is beside the point. Every serious student of the Word of God first seeks to discover its meaning...and then, and only then, to bring practice into conformity with it. Biblical principles determine Biblical practice, and the principle of silence was the principle of the first century church."* (The Role of Women In The Church," Charles Ryrie, Moody Press, Chicago, 1970, p. 78)

Female leadership in the church is good and necessary, but *only* as it implies teaching and/or ruling over other women and children. This doesn't say women can't say *anything* in the church, just that their role is limited regarding exercising teaching or ruling authority over men (this does *not at all* suggest an inadequacy in intelligence or worth).

There are some major churches today, who are wandering from this teaching, instead of correcting it. They suggest that we should not make an issue out of it, because we don't want to offend the un-churched and keep them from receiving Christ.

We are **not** called, however, to *vacillate* on Scriptural principles on the basis of whether or not *unbelievers* will be attracted to the Gospel. Our standard is to please God first. Then, if there is a *reasonable* need to soften the context (not the message) for evangelistic need, we have freedom to do so. But this should always be done in *wisdom.* I really do understand the principle that methods can and should change, while the message remains constant. But, I *also* know that too often the message has been clouded, because the method has been compromised. *In other words, the tail should never wag the dog!*

- *Roles In Society* -

This is the area of what's masculine and what's feminine, and these lifestyle implications or expectations should be guideposts for all of us. To begin with, sexual roles are not meant to be Biblical *straight-jackets*, where anyone who's a bit too feminine or a bit too masculine is to be considered gay or undesirable. But, the point still remains that God *has* created the sexes with *fundamental biological differences*. This means that we should **follow the implications** of these differences as a wise lifestyle strategy. This just makes good sense. To do the opposite is to foster "social re-engineering," which so many are doing in our culture today without apology (even in the church). The results have been devastating!

Overall, males are physically stronger and larger than females. Their bone and muscle structure, lung and circulatory capacities exceed those of their female counterparts and are overall more powerful. In physically demanding types of work or in sports, for instance, females will not be able on average to compete with the opposite sex...it's a fact of life and biology.

A while ago a top ranking female golfer played in an all-male tournament was blown away. Now, I'm sure she beat some of the men, but she was clearly dominated by most. It was simply a matter of physical strength. She could probably putt as well as many, but her fairway distances just couldn't compete. Such physical distinctions should offer wise men and women some practical implications, if they wish to be *true to the intent of God* on a societal level.

Also, women are more relationally and emotionally "fine-tuned" than men. This fits with their physical ability to give birth, nurse and nurture their children. Her sexuality is far more complex, no matter how much society tries to blur its distinctiveness. Her monthly cycle reminds her of this, her deeper relational needs complement this, and her greater need for intimacy during sex supports this. Men, on the other hand, have no such physical cycle, have far less a need for relationship and can easily be aroused and satisfied quickly, without much intimacy.

The Biblically espoused role for the man is to ensure provision and protection for his family, and this has always been a natural match for his physiology, as well. Only recently, due to major industrial and technical changes in the workplace, have these differences been softened. But, God's principles are eternal. Man has been given a calling; he is to provide for his family, regardless of the changes in the work environment (historically, this has always been the case as well). Biblically speaking, it was Adam, who primarily tilled the ground, while Eve fulfilled the relational and supportive role given to her for the children.

> *"Then the Lord God took the man and put him into the garden of Eden to cultivate it and keep it."* (Gen. 2:15)
>
> *"Then the Lord God said, "It is not good for the man to be alone; I will make him a helper suitable for him." (Gen. 2:18)*

Eve had no assigned role responsibilities as provider/protector. She was created as a "suitable helper" to relationally support her husband and *his* calling (notice how feminists have tried to do away with wives taking on their husband's last name). A woman's body and emotionally fine-tuned make-up have *uniquely equipped* her for this important task, and the historical record of both secular and religious society attests to this primary calling and advantage.

Application #1: Work

Because man was originally intended to be the provider/protector, he should model this in his lifestyle. Because woman was created and called to be the family nurturer, she should model this priority.

Men who stay at home <u>by choice</u> and let their wives pursue the higher paying or more stable careers, do so, I believe, in opposition to God's Word. Unusual financial setbacks, difficulties or loss of jobs can cause temporary role changes, which are understandable, of course. But, a *permanent* reversal of role responsibilities *by choice* (or passive choice) is at issue here.

I would suggest that women, who seek full-time career paths while raising children, review their motives for doing so, for such is not the *clear* teaching of God's Word. Simply desiring to pursue a career is also *not sufficient reason on its own to do so.*

> *"Therefore, I want younger widows to get married, bear children, keep house, and give the enemy no occasion for reproach."* (I Tim. 5:14 NIV)

On balance, however, Proverbs 31 does say that a godly woman can actively pursue income-making endeavors to assist her family's financial needs. In this passage, she is known as one who makes things to sell in the marketplace in order to return a profit for her family. So, even though some limited activity in the workplace may not appear to offend the Biblical role for a woman, she should still be identified and involved as the *primary family nurturer and care-giver in her home.* If the children are mostly grown up or if the couple is childless, then I don't necessarily see where full-time career employment would offend any Biblical standard.

However, I would suggest that if the relationship suffers from authority disagreements over money, hours, career moves, etc., that the husband and wife should carefully revisit their respective roles and responsibilities. These issues and their resolution *must* still rest within the leadership scope of the husband and support his primary role as the provider/protector and loving leader, not the reverse. In addition, a working wife should *always* choose a career path where her feminine distinctives and values can flourish and be appreciated. In this regard, please keep in mind that assertiveness, boldness, physical strength and competitiveness are *not* female traits, rather male, *regardless of a particular woman's proclivities or background.* Believers must endeavor to follow *as much as possible* what are the wisest and clearest Scriptural principles, not just an individual's physical and/or personality traits.

Role Application #2: Social concerns

In one's general lifestyle, men and women should model the intent of God as demonstrated in their physical and emotional differences.

- Dress -

"A woman must not wear men's clothing, nor a man wear women's clothing, for the LORD your God detests anyone who does this." (Deut. 22:5)

There should always be a reasonable *distinction* in appearance and dress between the sexes. It's not so much a matter of what is worn specifically as much as what male and female distinctives are fostered. I'm not talking about absolutes, here, but a reasonable application of wisdom. Enough said.

- Sports -

Regarding sports, what Title IX has done to women and their role in this country is unbelievable. Women are now **encouraged** to work out, build muscle, be aggressive, and to mentally and physically do everything in order to win, even competing with men. The lingo, the "get tough" mentality, the "no-pain-no-gain" attitude and all-out competitive trimmings that men have built up are now being fed to these young girls' minds. *That's role reversal in the making for it turns everything that is uniquely feminine into everything that is uniquely masculine.* Please don't believe for a moment that it doesn't affect them, their attitudes toward femininity, their sexual choices, their marriage relationships and the future psycho-sexual framework of the children they raise!

Regarding the concept of femininity, notice what the Apostle Peter says **God admires** and wants for women in I Peter 3:1-4:

> "...let it be the hidden person of the heart, with the imperishable quality of a gentle and quiet spirit, which is precious in the sight of God."

Unfortunately, women are paraded on television today as super heroes, who kick, punch, flip and fight other men as equals. First of all, this is nonsense, for most women couldn't begin to do this even with modest training, though occasionally I suppose some might. But, when a woman does commit her body to be trained and her attitudes to be "re-tooled" into aggressive and competitive co-equals with males, she not only offends "what is precious in the sight of God," but again fosters cultural blurring. The devastation this has caused in society would have made the 80's show, "Charlie's Angels," blush profusely!

If anyone who is a believer really thinks that muscle bound women strutting their stuff in competition can co-exist with their biological distinctives, then I would ask you to think deeper. And, if you further think "Will and Grace" type, cutesy and effeminate homosexual men are fun to watch on TV and are okay in God's sight...again, I believe you have been misled. God certainly doesn't hate homosexuals, but he does condemn *all behaviors* that aren't congruent with his will. Blurring sexual roles and laughing at such distortions must truly anger him, just as it did when Sodom traveled down the same sexually misguided road.

I know that some reading this book will say that my thoughts on biblical roles are archaic, perhaps chauvinistic. In response, I would ask you to read and *study* the Scriptures again. In addition, take a broad look at recent history and the results of role disintegration. I believe that if you do, you'll come to appreciate my thoughts here. If you still don't agree, then take what is reasonable to you in light of God's Word and apply it to your life. But, please be tolerant of those who are more conservative. Again, all of us will have to give account to our Lord for what we've believed and taught. Perhaps this is why Jesus said the following to his disciples:

> "I am sending you out like sheep among wolves. Therefore be as shrewd as snakes and as innocent as doves." (Matt. 10:16)

Your Spiritual Tool Box

Today's Project:
Sexual Distinctiveness

Your Blueprint:

"...I want the men everywhere to pray, lifting up holy hands without anger or disputing. I also want the women to dress modestly, with decency and propriety, adorning themselves, not with elaborate hairstyles or gold or pearls or expensive clothes, but with good deeds, appropriate for women who profess to worship God. A woman should learn in quietness and full submission. I do not permit a woman to teach or to assume authority over a man; she must be quiet. For Adam was formed first, then Eve. And Adam was not the one deceived; it was the woman who was deceived and became a sinner. But women will be saved through childbearing—if they continue in faith, love and holiness with propriety."

Keeping It Plumb:

Femininity is gentle and submissive in nature, does not value physical prowess or strength, and it excels in intimate relationships and family nurturing. Masculinity values competitive and aggressive challenges, seeks to acquire physical strength, and excels in achieving life security for self and family.

Who's Holding Your Ladder

I heard this expression just the other day and thought it powerful enough to pass on. In a world of difficulty and challenge, all of us need someone strong and reliable holding our life ladder and making steady and safe. Spiritually speaking, the simplest answer is that God should be at the bottom, steadying our life ladder.

However, it is important to recognize that God provides his support by various means. If you had a prophet as a friend in Old Testament days, you would feel pretty safe. If something went wrong or you needed some special grace of some sort, you'd give a call to Elijah and ask for a miracle. And, if it was God's will, you could count on your request being answered momentarily. However, God works quite differently today…here's some examples.

- You're been putting off getting those expensive new tires for your car. At the men's Bible study, one of the guys gives you $200 and says he's feels God wanted him to help you out, even though he didn't know why.
- Your bank notifies you that there is an extra $1000 in your savings due to a mistake they made 2 years ago, but it was caught in a recent audit. The next day, your refrigerator calls it quits…replacement cost…$950!
- You're teaching a Sunday school lesson and present something on the topic of patience. It seemed like nothing was special in it, but the next day, John, who's in your class, tells you it was a critical help to him. He says, "I didn't know what to do, and God spoke to me through you yesterday. Thanks so much."

In all these ways above, God either answered prayers or moved in someone's life without an obvious, "supernatural" manifestation. Each thing God did was purposeful and causal and would not have happened apart from the intercessory hand of God intervening in someone's life. Still, though each one happened within the realm of "natural physical laws," each one also occurred with intentional choice on the part of our sovereign Lord. No fire, lightening, earthquakes or healing accompanied these events, yet God proved himself to be real and caring.

So, we may never "see" God working by experiencing some sort of miraculous manifestation, but that doesn't mean he's not very busy behind the lines. He's carefully stepping into our daily walk to coordinate events, as he faithfully holds our ladder securely in its place.

"And we know that in all things God works for the good of those who love him, who have been called according to his purpose." (Romans 8:28)

Though God is always holding the ladder, this also doesn't mean that he controls every event in such a way as to eliminate our responsibility to make proper choices. Understanding where the personal will of man begins and the sovereign and purposeful will of God enters is a mystery for sure, even though believers have been trying to discern the difference for millennia. But, let me offer some general guidelines that help.

WE SOMETIMES ROCK THE LADDER OURSELVES

Theologically speaking, all of us exist in a life situation referred to in the Bible as the "state of sin." This means that everything has been damaged to some degree by the ravaging disease of sin, including both creature and creation. Our inner natures possess an *impassioned bent* toward self-centered and sensually-based behaviors at the expense of love and purity before God. Even the world around us groans with the pangs of immanent disaster and death.

A friend of mine was on his ladder working on the over-hanging gutters of his house, when the ladder slipped. He fell only a few feet, but the fall cracked his hip, which had to be replaced. He would be the first to say that he didn't use enough wisdom to be up there in the first place, perhaps hiring someone younger to fix the gutters would have been better. So, all of us are "caught up" in this world of sin, and it affects the physical, mental and spiritual environment around us. Our lifestyle can be rocked significantly by our own choices, attitudes and lifestyle.

GOD SOMETIMES ROCKS THE LADDER

There are times when God is causally and pre-determinedly rocking our ladder. Perhaps he may do this in order to get our attention, and awaken us from a desensitized spirit and/or lifestyle. Or, he may want to "tear us down in order to build us up," as a familiar song emphasizes, preparing us for a season of special growth or ministry. Whatever his purposes, our Lord does know how to open our hearts and minds by very graphic, sometimes painful ways, when he sees it as necessary for our good.

I remember a time when I was biking home on a rainy day around dusk through an area with a lot of homes. I was riding down the side walk on a side road where the speed limit was about 30 mph and started to cross a smaller street. Coming the other way was a fast-moving car, and the driver cut in front of me with no blinker or pause…he just swerved onto the street I was crossing. Well, he hit me half way through the street, stopping the bike and sending me head over heels into the air over the car's hood. In the darkness, I couldn't see a thing and spun around in the air, then landed on my posterior with one foot on the street and one up on the curve. I "somehow" had missed a fire hydrant, a road sign and a stop sign directly in front of me and had no serious cuts or injuries. As I sat there, trying to assess my situation, I prayed and thanked God for his mercy. Later on, I evaluated the "why" of the situation, realizing that I was ignoring some significant sin going on in my life. My "Ladder-Holder" was speaking loudly to me in order for me to make some necessary changes in my life.

TALK WITH THE LADDER HOLDER

As believers, God is at the bottom of our ladder bringing stability and wise counsel. But, if we're not listening to what he's saying as we move through our daily lives, we'll miss his instructions and strategic coaching. Prayer is a significant activity for all of us as we climb daily ladders, address important life tasks and fulfill our responsibilities. Combined with a faithful study of God's Word, we can learn to recognize the Lord's counsel and act quickly enough to avoid unnecessary falls and unwise antics on the ladder of daily living.

> *"Leave your simple ways and you will live;*
> *walk in the way of insight."* (Prov. 9:6)

Your Spiritual Tool Box

Today's Project:
Decisions & Directions

Your Blueprint:
*"Trust in the Lord with all your heart,
and do not lean on your own understanding.
In all your ways acknowledge him,
and he will make straight your paths."*
(Proverbs 2:5,6 ESV)

Keeping It Plumb:

It may be painful to fall off a ladder, but it must be unbearable to fall off the ladder *of life*. Those that don't know Christ personally live their lives in the confidence, or lack of it, in what they are and what they do. That's risky business, frankly, for many non-believers experience some terrible life circumstances simply because they refuse to let God into their lives. Then, when problems overwhelm them, they fall to the ground because of unending stress, financial bankruptcy, relational breakups, job loss, etc. Believers are also involved in a somewhat precarious climb at times, but they trust God to keep their ladder secure and look to him for necessary strength when the climb gets difficult and dangerous. Let God into your decisions and into your difficulties; seek his will in all circumstances and you'll find his enabling grace sufficient in everything.

"But...It Feels So Good!"

"By faith Moses, when he was grown up, refused to be called the son of Pharaoh's daughter, choosing rather to be mistreated with the people of God than to enjoy the fleeting pleasures of sin. He considered the reproach of Christ greater wealth than the treasures of Egypt, for he was looking to the reward..." Heb. 11:25

As the picture above shows, relaxing on a sandy, sunny beach in south Florida really does feel good! Life's full of opportunities to just sit back and enjoy the feelings of a cool breeze, a warming sun or a refreshing dip in the ocean. The important thing is, however, that the pleasure in which we indulge our physical and emotional senses is not outside of the will of God. Just because we enjoy something that "feels good" doesn't mean it's necessarily okay to do so. Here's some examples.

Mary was upset with her friend Martha a football game where both of their kids were playing, though on opposite teams (both are believers). When Martha's son made a touchdown, it was Mary's son that didn't block him well enough and let him sneak over the line to score. Martha shouted out, "That's the way, pound those "₈&·◆♏︎≈" idiots into the ground...that blocker's afraid of you...he's just an idiot anyway!" Martha was upset over Martha calling her son a cowardly idiot, and she deeply resented her for saying so...not to mention being appalled by the bad language. Martha apologized later, saying that at the time she was just caught up in the emotion.

Bill struggles with fantasizing about a particular woman at work. Though he's happily married, the woman just "turns him on," as he tells his Pastor. Bill is at church seeking help from the Pastor on how to control is thought life. "I know it's wrong, but, hey, I'm not having an affair, or something," he says. "But, I just find it hard to control my mind. She's just so attractive and…well...we really get along so great!"

Teenager Tommy Smith is stuck on a high, but it's not Jesus…it's heroin. "It's so cheap," he says to his friend Sawyer, "that you can get it anywhere. My home life's a mess, I'm graduating this year and I just don't know where I'm going. I can't stand my parents, and I'm confused about God and stuff. And, this stuff makes me feel so good!"

These are just three simple examples where people struggle with desire to think or do things that are "feel good" indulgences crying out for satisfaction. They're often just momentary "sin pills" to remove the temporary pain we're feeling inside over some sort of difficulty. Other times, they can be habitual strains of desire and/or emotion that have rooted themselves within us over the years or since childhood. But, the bottom line is, they feel good enough to cause us to leave God's will at the door and enter the house of sinful pleasure. Eventually, of course, they bring their own degree of pain and punishment, especially for the Christian. Often, this only enhances the need for either taking a "bigger sin pill" to satisfy our ever-growing desires, or our spiritual lapses simply destroy us from within. Neither is a pretty picture.

So, sin feels good. But, here's answer to all of us who struggle from time to time with things that feel good, but are spiritually harmful and disloyal to Christ. *We've got to want God and his Will more than sin and its pleasures.* Now, that answer is not complicated, but it's not meant to be an over-simplified response to a profound issue, either. Still, it's the bottom-line solution to any such issue.

In the above examples, Martha justifies her "mouthy diatribe" by saying she was just caught up in the emotion. No kidding. But, that's what happens when we want something more than the will of God. She wanted to say what she did, no one forced her to say it. It was a "verbal sports killing," if you will, that she allowed instead of wanting to curb her emotions, reign them in and respond with a due sense of self-control befitting to her Christian commitment. I'm sure that our Savior would enjoy watching a competitive game, but he would show restraint and respect while doing so. Again, Martha's actions satisfied her human nature at the time, plain and simple.

Bill is struggling with sheer physical and emotional desire for a person of the opposite sex. It's a natural and godly reaction, but God's wants us to avoid all such mental and physical satisfaction until marriage. And, in this case, Bill is married and doesn't have another option, so why is he fishing in such an obviously sinful pond? Well, he's enjoying it...again...and again, plain and simple. Regardless of whether such things are being satisfied at home, regardless of his particular personality issues from his early childhood experiences, regardless of...well...of anything else, he must ask himself a critical question. "What do I want the most? Should I please myself with moments of lust, or should I please God with sexual purity? Is toying with this urge mentally worth the loss of the spiritual intimacy and the providential blessing of God in my life?" Because, that's what the cost will be on some level. And, it could develop into something much worse.

Tommy Smith is simply enjoying the euphoric feelings from a drug-induced high. That high has probably gotten more expensive and more habitual since he began dousing the painful embers of his dis-functional family relationships. The first few bites into his drug appetite were on his part, but now the drugs have bitten him back with a vengeance to the point of no return. Bottom line? It's so pleasurable and stress releasing that he simply has little will power left to ignore the self-satisfying cravings that cry out from deep inside his heart.

Okay, let's look at the answer again, which is determining to want God and his will more than satisfying our feelings, our lusts and our euphoric highs. No amount of simple positive attitudes, pious platitudes or mental games will turn these desires away. Only a stronger, more deeply rooted and satisfying desire will slay the Goliath within these people.

For believers, change won't come by simply *saying* you want God more than anything else. It must come from the heart, the source of our deepest and most impassioned self. The situation is similar to the relationship between faith and works in salvation. Good works can't save us, but they reveal a genuine, life changing faith. Similarly, deeply and passionate desire for God ultimately reveals itself when we turn fully from habitual sin. It's the primary road to winning.

So, in Hebrews 11:26, the motivating reality that drove Moses was recognizing how temporary were the passing pleasures of Egyptian royalty. It would be better and *more satisfying*, he recognized, to follow God's perfect will and his challenging call for a life among his own people.

Do you see the impassioned faith Moses acquired? Do you sense the desire burning within his heart and mind for the things of God? Do you feel the life-changing drive for holiness that gripped him and turned him from carnal indulgence to spiritual hunger? Do you see how motivated he was to seek God and his blessing?

The more you and I understand and experience the incomparable joys of spiritual purity and the providential blessing of walking with Jesus, the more we will be willing to throw away our lust-driven toys. Our relationship with God and the rewards of obedience will effectively and consistently pull our hearts away from evil to freely embrace the Spirit's love for God resident within us. And, of course, I say this with *great feeling!*

Your Spiritual Tool Box

Today's Project:
Feelings And Your Future

Your Blueprint:
"Set your minds on things that are above, not on things that are on earth. For you have died, and your life is hidden with Christ in God. When Christ who is your life appears, then you also will appear with him in glory." (Col. 3:2-4 ESV)

Keeping It Plumb:
Living for Jesus a life that is true;
Striving to please him in all that I do,
yielding allegiance, glad hearted and free,
this is the pathway of blessing for me.
Refrain:
O Jesus, Lord and Savior, I give myself to thee;
for thou, in thy atonement, didst give thyself for me;
I own no other master, my heart shall be thy throne,
My life I give, henceforth to live, O Christ for thee alone.
[Living For Jesus: Words by Thomas O. Chisholm, music by Carl H. Lowden]

*"Life isn't about doing what feels good;
It's about doing what is good."*

Who's Driving?

"You can't do that?" responded the project manager at NASA.

"Yes, we can!" returned Roger, a bright young physicist, who was just recently hired. "Look, we've been to the moon, and we've dropped vehicles on Mars. Let's go to the sun for our next project."

"Impossible." said the project manager, "No one's ever come up with an intelligent plan yet to do that successfully." Everyone in the briefing room nodded their heads in agreement.

"Listen, ladies and gentlemen, I don't have doctoral degrees in Molecular Science, Astro-Physics and Bio-Chemistry for nothing! I've thought it through and through, and I know it can be done. Just listen." The other NASA physicists and engineers were dumbfounded and waited expectedly for Roger's solution for landing on the hot ball of gaseous light we call the sun.

"It's simple. We'll land at night."

So much for intelligence. But, seriously, each of us is driven by something. Roger was driven by intellect, though not very well. Nevertheless, intellectual understanding of life is a driving force for many, and they become teachers, scientists and professors of colleges. Others, however, are driven by achievement and accomplishment, perhaps becoming great entrepreneurs, corporate presidents, lawyers or politicians. Still others are driven by people and relationships, hoping to please or help others in some way. Many from this perspective become doctors, ministers and social workers. All of us are driven by bodily, attitudinal and behavioral "drivers," but we are accountable to God for how we satisfy them. Whatever the driving force is within each of us, it's important as believers that we watch over our "drivers" in order to control and/or channel such things instead of being controlled by them.

The reason I mention this, is that the Christian life is not just about pursuing our own inclinations and intentions. As believers, we recognize God's right to lead and direct us towards his plan for our lives. Now, that can certainly be in line with how he's "wired us," of course, and that understanding is an important clue to follow. For instance, many fine and capable people have ended up in a completely different career or ministry focus in which they began, due to changes in the marketplace, personal issues, family concerns and God's purposeful will. So, we must begin by looking at how God has equipped us, but we must always be *fundamentally* open to God's leading. A familiar verse for this is Proverbs 3:5,6:

> "Trust in the LORD with all your heart And do not lean on your own understanding. In all your ways acknowledge Him, And He will make your paths straight."

I remember talking with three guys at a men's Bible study/picnic on a hot summer night. One was a factory worker for an GM, another a respected wood working professional and another held various jobs over the years. All three said they thought they were being called to the ministry, so I asked why. The GM worker was just a great Christian guy, who was very active in the church, was an Elder, teacher and youth leader. So, he had a lot of spiritual motivation and church experience that would realistically "incline" him toward the Pastorate. The furniture maker, who had fantastic skills doing what he did, had no experience in ministry except as a helper with cooking and other organizational things in various church activities. The last gentlemen just "felt" called to help people and preach. He was sort of a country type guy, I believe, with no education beyond high school. So, here they were, feeling called to ministry because of sermons and missionary teaching to which they had recently been exposed. They were godly guys, sincere and open.

Now, let's move the clock ahead 10 years later. The GM guy got some Bible School education and entered Pastoral ministry in a 250 member church. But, he had some personal issues that cropped up and collapsed his ministry future. He eventually went into real estate, made good money and now is also a well-respected Chaplain for a national ministry to corporate America. His drive to minister to others was genuine, though temporarily interrupted. God took care of him and his family, and moved into something in better alignment with his basic spiritual drive to help others.

The furniture worker never rigorously pursued ministry, and eventually became divorced. The country guy did pursue ministry after some brief Bible School studies, but only held a couple of church positions in some small church congregations (not to diminish smaller churches, of course). He ultimately returned to various types of work in order to provide for his family.

It's amazing to me how all of us at times "feel" our way toward this or that career or toward some other life situation. Nothing wrong with feelings, but they can change and, therefore, are not very solid things to build upon for career and ministry. Getting a "call" to serve in ministry is also one of those areas that has been abused, for too many have picked up the wrong phone.

As a career counselor, I recognize that assessing one's skills and one's motivations are very important considerations, when seeking a successful profession. But, life is not often so simple. It sometimes asks us to make decisions in the absence of crystal clear direction from God. In those situations, a person needs wisdom and discernment to maneuver through the fog of uncertainty and clouded vision. This is not only true in the area of career focus, but also when handling our attitudinal and behavioral drives as well.

One of my favorite musical plays is "Phantom of the Opera," performed for years in Toronto, Canada. One scene portrays two people "floating" along in a small boat through an eerie and scary swamp. One person is holding out a small lantern at the front of the boat, trying to peer through the dense fog in search of the Phantom (as I remember it). That's how I perceive to be the will of God in certain circumstances…uncertain of what lies ahead, yet something in which I must go forward carefully until God reveals a different plan.

The difficulty in all this is being able to discriminate between all the "drivers" that may be pushing at our hearts at any given time in order to identify God's will. The three guys in the backyard on that humid summer night were trying to sense the will of God for their lives. As their story shows, sometimes we are correct in choosing a course of action that is the will of God, but we falter in some way and need to seek God's direction for another path. Other times, we are mistaken in interpreting God's Will, yet unwisely plunge ahead, because we want what we want so much. And, some decisions in life do not amount to a "right or wrong" situation…we are simply free to choose what is best on our own.

I should take a few minutes to touch upon *moral* drivers, too. Not only must we decide what is best for our career choices, but there are drivers within us that crave satisfaction in attitudinal and behavior choices.

My first room-mate at college came from Florida. In that time period, there was far more prejudice toward blacks than today, even among believers. In fact, his church was more segregated than one would suppose. He'd say, "Well, they just live and get along with each other, and we (whites) do the same. We don't fight or try to be unkind to each other, we just live separated lives, that's all. That's the way it is down here." Life certainly has changed since then.

The point is that my room-mate's thinking was skewed and not Christian. His spiritual "driver" wasn't just that whites and blacks should live in separate cultures. In reality, I'd say his "driver" was prejudicial thinking, that whites were better people, more acceptable and more valuable to God, even if ever so slightly. That's a "driver" that can run very deep in some people (in either direction, of course).

We also have strong "drivers" that pull or push at us in personal areas regarding sex, food, entertainment, friendships, etc. Jesus wants us to acknowledge any desire that seeks to control us and to satisfy it *only* within the parameters of God's will.

I remember one couple in church that had had a rough time getting along with each other through the years. They finally decided to seek divorce, rationalizing that God would forgive them for separating. "At least we can have a fresh start with someone else." (there was no unfaithfulness involved). I'm sure many things were driving them toward divorce...anger, loss of desire, financial frustration, etc. – but, for sure, it wasn't God's Spirit driving them toward divorce...that was their choice.

So, let's ask ourselves an important question: "What is driving us to do the things we do...personally, professionally, spiritually? Here are some helpful guidelines I have acquired for healthy decision making.

- A "career driver" may or may not be aligned with God's will. We feel and/or desire many different things, so be careful about saying with certainty what is or is not regarding God's will for your career. Search methodically and carefully for God's direction, along with much prayer and wise counsel.
- All "behavioral drivers" may or may not be godly or morally acceptable. Sexual satisfaction is a godly "driver," but how we channel that desire into attitudes and behaviors is fundamental to acquiring spiritual maturity. All such inclinations must be clearly aligned with God's will as revealed in the Bible. If

our desires and determinations are antagonistic to godliness and/or abusive to godly wisdom or Scripture, such inclinations become outside of God's will.
- There's often a lot going on inside of us of which we only scratch the service. In all decisions, let's *prayerfully search* for God's *wisdom* in the Bible and seek the *insights* of others whose counsel we respect. It's much easier *to avoid consequences* than it is to *clean up after them.*

Your Spiritual Tool Box

Today's Project:
Who's In YOUR Driver's Seat?

Your Blueprint:
"Search me, O God, and know my heart; Try me and know my anxious thoughts; And see if there be any hurtful way in me, And lead me in the everlasting way.
(Psalm 139:24 NASB)

Keeping It Plumb:
It was a beautiful day, as my wife and I drove out of the college driveway onto the country road that led us toward home. We enjoyed taking the day to visit our Alma Mata, Houghton College, which is situated in upstate New York about an hour from our home. Unfortunately, we decided to use our own "geographic instincts" for the trip home, thinking we were familiar enough with the area (we hadn't been there in years!). Three hours later, after passing through Amish country and going up and down mountainous dirt roads, we found ourselves very much lost! But, we eventually asked enough people along the way to get us back on course, and finally pulled into our driveway.

It's not much different with God's will. If we give into our own motivational and intentional drivers, we can cause havoc in our spiritual lives. Better to let Christ rule within and to direct our inner person through life's challenges. Practically speaking, arriving in heaven will be fantastic, but avoiding rock-strewn, rutted and pot-holed dirt roads on the way there isn't the best road to travel!

Abigail's Wisdom

"Now then, my children, listen to me;
blessed are those who keep my ways.
Listen to my instruction and be wise;
do not disregard it.
Blessed are those who listen to me,
watching daily at my doors,
waiting at my doorway.
For those who find me find life
and receive favor from the Lord."
Proverbs 8:32-36

Wisdom is a precious commodity, according to the Bible, and not everyone has it or seeks it. But, those who do, find blessing and favor from the Lord. Scripture from Genesis through Revelation distinguishes between two types of people, the godly and the ungodly, those that fear the Lord and those that don't. Those that are godly and reverently fear God are counted as truly wise people, for who would not want to be favored by Almighty God?

Fundamentally speaking, therefore, a mature believer in Jesus Christ will be someone who seeks to be a man or woman of wisdom. But, what is wisdom? According to the passage above, it is someone who *listens* to God (his commandments and spiritual principles) and who *keeps* them with consistency. Please notice that wisdom is not the same as knowledge, rather it is the application of what one knows that makes one wise.

People are drawn to someone who has discernment, understanding and wisdom. They seek out such a person, because they know that there is sensible counsel upon their lips. Life can be very difficult at times and wisdom is needed to chase away the clouds of confusion and replace them with a bit of spiritual sunshine and good sense.

Abagail was just such a person in the life of King David. Actually, she came into his life just before he became king and saved him from a dishonorable act of revenge upon her husband. He was running from King Saul with his band of men, when her husband, Nabal, acted without respect for who David was.

> "While David was in the wilderness, he heard that Nabal was shearing sheep. So, he sent ten young men and said to them, "'Go up to Nabal at Carmel and greet him in my name. Say to him: 'Long life to you! Good health to you and your household! And good health to all that is yours! 'Now I hear that it is sheep-shearing time. When your shepherds were with us, we did not mistreat them, and the whole time they were at Carmel nothing of theirs was missing. Ask your own servants and they will tell you. Therefore, be favorable toward my men, since we come at a festive time. Please give your servants and your son David whatever you can find for them.' "

But, Nabal responded in pride, and he rejected David's plea, sending his men away in disgrace. David was angry to the point of revenge and gathered his mighty warriors to return and kill Nabal. Nabal's wife, Abigail, interceded and softened David's anger.

> "Abigail acted quickly. She took two hundred loaves of bread, two skins of wine, five dressed sheep, five seahs of roasted grain, a hundred cakes of raisins and two hundred cakes of pressed figs, and loaded them on donkeys. Then she told her servants, 'Go on ahead; I'll follow you.' But she did not tell her husband Nabal...When Abigail saw David, she quickly got off her donkey and bowed down before David with her face to the ground. She fell at his feet and said: 'Pardon your servant, my lord, and let me speak to you; hear what your servant has to say. Please pay no attention, my lord, to that wicked man Nabal. He is just like his name— his name means Fool, and folly goes with him. And as for me, your servant, I did not see the men my lord sent. And now, my lord, as surely as the Lord your God lives and as you live, since the Lord has kept you from bloodshed and from avenging yourself with your own hands, may

your enemies and all who are intent on harming my lord be like Nabal. And let this gift, which your servant has brought to my lord, be given to the men who follow you.......'"

So, David found Abigail's plea a just and compassionate one, and she responded in kind.

"David said to Abigail, 'Praise be to the Lord, the God of Israel, who has sent you today to meet me. May you be blessed for your good judgment and for keeping me from bloodshed this day and from avenging myself with my own hands. Otherwise, as surely as the Lord, the God of Israel, lives, who has kept me from harming you, if you had not come quickly to meet me, not one male belonging to Nabal would have been left alive by daybreak.......'"

When Nabal heard about the incident and how close he had come to his own demise, he fell over dead.

"Then David sent word to Abigail, asking her to become his wife. His servants went to Carmel and said to Abigail, 'David has sent us to you to take you to become his wife.'"

So, everything turned out for good for both Abigail and David. But, Nabal, a man referred to as a fool by his own wife, was a man whose death was self-inflicted due to a severe lack of sensibility and wisdom. He used poor judgment and paid the ultimate price for it.

Application:

Wise people are people who **watch** for wisdom. In other words, they value it so greatly that they continually search for its truths and principles. They do not "disregard" it, as Nabal did, but rather reach out to embrace it as a welcomed friend.

The primary place we search for it is in the **Scriptures,** for God's Word is always reliable and trustworthy. The book of Proverbs is particularly full of meaty sayings and principles that, when followed, are guideposts toward success in life. The New Testament is also loaded to the brim with precepts and principles, which can safely coach us around unnecessary dangers and spiritual pitfalls.

Wisdom is also found as one goes to God in **prayer,** asking for it in sincerity and truth. The Holy Spirit greatly desires this spiritual pursuit and rewards those who ask Him for wisdom, when asked in the attitude of faith.

"If any of you lacks wisdom, you should ask God, who gives generously to all without finding fault, and it will be given to you." (James 1:5)

In addition, **life itself** is a resource of truth and wisdom for those willing to learn from it, for, *"Out in the open wisdom calls aloud, she raises her voice in the public square."* (Prov. 1:20) In this context, then, failure is a good teacher, *if* one accepts the responsibility to learn from one's mistakes. Unfortunately, those who are ego-driven and proud do not learn from this important reservoir of resource and do not receive favor from God. Life may be speaking to them, but they have *closed ears*.

> *"But he gives us more grace. That is why Scripture says: 'God opposes the proud but shows favor to the humble.'"* (James 4:6)

Overall, wisdom isn't something lying around that you just happen to stumble upon, saying, "Oh, look what I found!" To the contrary, wisdom is something one must seek with honest and energetic intent, if one is to successfully discover it, which is the idea found above in "watching" for it.

> *"For if you cry for discernment, lift your voice for understanding; If you seek her as silver And search for her as for hidden treasures; Then you will discern the fear of the LORD And discover the knowledge of God...."* (Prov. 2:3-5)

Notice also that wisdom is something that is also found by "waiting" and "listening." In other words, there's no McDonald's answer to much of life's challenges. Fast food is great on occasion, but "fast food wisdom" can't be ordered up at the counter of spiritual truth. It can be encountered, for instance, when hearing a wise person speak, or by reading Scripture or by hearing a good sermon. But, it can't be processed without "chewing" on it in your mind and "swallowing" it into your heart. Only when one takes time to understand and discern a given truth will one ingest wisdom deep enough to feed one's soul with life changing grace.

Years ago, I was looking out the kitchen window into the backyard at the rain-drenching winds moving across the trees. A storm had quickly come along, and its winds were reaching above 70 miles per hour, according to the weather service. It was a freaky thing, fast moving and powerful.

Next to the garage was a tool that I had left out, so I was deciding whether or not to venture out in the torrential rains to retrieve it. It wasn't going anywhere, frankly, but I thought it might be interesting to "feel the storm." So, I went out the back door and ran quickly to the spot next to the garage by one of the large oak trees, where the tool lay. Picking it up, I paused for a moment to look around in the wind and rain, then moved to go back. Pow! Just as I turned, a huge, 6-inch thick limb crashed down on the very spot I had been only 3 seconds before! I ran back to the house as quickly as I could...wet, cold, shaking and very thankful.

Wisdom can be learned through insight or stupidity. In this case, it was simple stupidity, in the face of God's mercy and grace, that taught me to forgo youthful inquisitiveness. It could have been a more painful, even a life-threatening experience, employed by the Lord to enlarge my capacity of discernment. Please remember, again, that wisdom can be learned the easy way, or the hard way. That stormy lesson showed me which way fundamentally makes the most sense.

Your Spiritual Tool Box

Today's Project:
Discernment and Discretion

Your Blueprint:
"And it is my prayer that your love may abound more and more, with knowledge and all discernment, so that you may approve what is excellent, and so be pure and blameless for the day of Christ..."
(Phil. 1:9-10)

Keeping It Plumb:
Christians ought to be the most sensible and seasoned people on earth. We love God, and we have his inerrant Word to study and follow. Could anyone ask for anything better? There's a key, though, and that's taking the time, like Abagail, to "think things through before acting things out." That gives God enough time to impress upon us what is better and best for our decisions and life destinations.

"The fear of the Lord is the beginning of wisdom"
(Pr. 9:10)

Pain and Gain

Have you ever watched a glass-blower (glass-smith or gaffer) work his skills? It's truly an amazing display of art and technique that produces some very beautiful pieces of colorful glassware. Recently, we travelled to Corning Glass in Elmira, New York and watched one craftsmen create some gorgeous pieces for sale in their stores.

Two things impress me with the process we saw. First, the immense skill involved and, second, the amount of heat necessary to mold the glass into a consistency that is useful. I believe these are also the two *fundamental* principles God uses in the refinement of our spiritual maturity. The more we are compliant with our spiritual Glass-smith, the more beautiful will be the final creation.

The Master's Skill

Joseph was a good man that had bad things happen to him. Thrown into a pit by his murderous and jealous brothers, he was ultimately removed and sold to a travelling caravan of merchants. He ended up in Egypt, working for a compassionate officer named Potiphar, who was the Captain of the Guards in Pharaoh's service. Potiphar recognized Joseph's capability and promoted him into significant service in the palace. Potiphar's wife then tried unsuccessfully to seduce Joseph, and in her anger, had her him thrown in prison for a period of years. Eventually, Joseph's reputation as an interpreter of dreams brought him into Pharaoh's court as the number-two-person in authority over all of Egypt. God then used him to bring needed resource to a famine ravaged world, while restoring his relationships with his repentant brothers.

Joseph went through a lot of personal pain and sorrow during those confusing years of undeserved dishonor and servitude, yet he never blamed God in bitterness. Looking back later at all of the pain, he said,

> *"As for you (e.g. his brothers), you meant evil against me, but God meant it for good, to bring it about that many people should be kept alive, as they are today."* (Genesis 50:20)

Pain…problems…pressures…we've all experienced these unwanted things here and there throughout our lives. But, pain is often a tool used by the Master to bring about significant changes for good in our spiritual lives. Now, sometimes the message is just plain common sense, with no particular lightning bolts splitting the heavens. For instance, if you swim in an area of the ocean known for its shark population, don't complain if you end up a tasty meal for one of them (you couldn't complain at that point anyway, right?!). Or, if you're eighty years old and try climbing a tree to show your grandson how "young" you are, well, the pain from a broken leg after falling is built into life; it's not necessarily a special revelation sent by the Lord.

On the other hand, God *can* and *does* use pain, problems and pressures specifically to school us, warn us and deepen us in our spiritual walk with him. He is actually very skilled in these techniques, and, just like the glassblower, he knows how much adversity to bring against us to mold us into spiritual compliance.

Dealing With Difficulty

Sometimes, and unlike Joseph, our pain, problems and pressures are self-inflicted, the result of poor choices, immaturities and outright sinful indulgence. But, even if they are not, we must still face these "dark intruders" wisely, without allowing simple difficulty…large or small…to rock our spiritual balance. This is never an easy task, even though Joseph provides us with a good picture of one who did it well. I would suggest the following process, when things get difficult.

Pray

When you're at the beginning of anything…*you begin*, so start out with prayer. Prayer is not necessarily something to understand, nor is it something to ignore when you're mad. It's an ongoing relationship with Christ, who is not surprised or caught unaware by our life challenges and/or difficulties. He may even be the *cause* of our difficulties at specific times, working his truth into our unhappy lives through some degree of difficulty or pain. But, whatever he is up to, you can be sure that it is for our good, for that is his promise – *"working in everything for good."* (Rom. 8:28) So, whether or not you understand everything you're praying about, nevertheless, always draw near to God in all circumstances of life.

Accept

Okay, this is the tough part. That's because acceptance has to come from the heart, if it's real. Many of us may sincerely mouth the words in our heads, "Yes, Lord, your will be done, even in this difficult time." But, only when it is spoken from the heart will God recognize it as a genuine act of surrender and worship. And, this is what pain does, it drives God's Truth deep into our hearts, where we truly and genuinely accept it. Yes, it hurting, unrelenting and seemingly unending, but if we let it do its work, good results can come from it.

As I'm writing this, I'm sitting at my computer with my right leg lifted up and resting on a stool. My foot has been swollen for two weeks, due to playing two sets of tennis immediately after 18 holes of golf. Now, the doctors can't seem to find any specific reason for it, other than over exertion, which certainly is something I need to hear, practically speaking. But, I'm also searching for a *possible* other reason for it. Is time needed for spiritual reflection, repentance, renewal or, perhaps, in preparation for a season of special ministry of some sort? I don't know, but I'm staying close to my Lord to see if there's an additional message, rather than just "slow down, man!" Here's a great verse in this context:

> *"I the LORD search the heart and examine the mind, to reward each person according to their conduct, according to what their deeds deserve."* (Jer. 17:10)

Could God be speaking to *your heart* in order to initiate some needed change? Here's some possibilities that he might be saying to you…some spiritual improvements you might consider. They highlight some deeper changes that Jesus may be asking of you to contemplate through the language of pain.

- Is he seeking *uncompromising* humility?
- Is he hoping for a more *un-deterrable* faith?
- Is he looking for more *authentic* commitment?
- Is he desiring *complete ownership* for your failures?
- Is he working within you for *whole-hearted* obedience?
- Is he developing an *impenetrable and immovable* mindset?

It is difficult to find God's specific will for our lives at times, for sure. Those that persevere and truly seek his counsel in the midst of it, however, will be rewarded.

"So many problems and pressures to meet;
Enable me, Jesus, to rest at your feet."

Include

Include others into your experience with whatever pain, problems or pressures that you are going through. Sharing with others and having them pray for you is not an option, or only something you do when needy. Part of God's purpose in fellowship is fulfilled when we pray for one another, and sometimes it may be the only road for healing that is available.

> *"Is anyone among you in trouble? Let them pray. Is anyone happy? Let them sing songs of praise. Is anyone among you sick? Let them call the elders of the church to pray over them and anoint them with oil in the name of the Lord. And the prayer offered in faith will make the sick person well; the Lord will raise them up. If they have sinned, they will be forgiven. Therefore, confess your sins to each other and pray for each other so that you may be healed. The prayer of a righteous person is powerful and effective."* (James 5:13-16)

Never complain

Finding help from others as well as garnering their support and/or encouragement does demand that we share our hurts with sincerity. But, it doesn't mean that we pour out our pain in the form of unnecessary negativity, spiteful condemnation, unending bitterness and constant complaining. Such stuff doesn't help in the long run and only hardens our hearts instead of softening them toward God's love. So, let the poison out of the wound, but afterwards avoid needless and continuing regurgitations and/or rehearsing of any issues and problems. "Faithing it through" the pain and difficulties of life, like it or not, is what God calls us to *genuinely* do. And, the rewards, both now and later, are worth the effort!

> *"Therefore, since we are surrounded by such a great cloud of witnesses, let us throw off everything that hinders and the sin that so easily entangles. And let us run with perseverance the race marked out for us, fixing our eyes on Jesus, the pioneer and perfecter of faith."* (Heb. 12:1, 2)

Your Spiritual Tool Box

Today's Project:
Listening To God Speak When It Hurts

Your Blueprint:
*"When there is a prophet among you,
I, the Lord, reveal myself to them in visions,
I speak to them in dreams.
But this is not true of my servant Moses;
he is faithful in all my house.
With him I speak face to face,
clearly and not in riddles;
he sees the form of the Lord.
Why then were you not afraid
to speak against my servant Moses?"*
(Numbers 12:7, 8)

Keeping It Plumb:

Speaking face to face with the Creator of the universe...wow! Until God ever gives *us* such an opportunity, we might first consider that he already does speak to us in many ways. He can speak through circumstances, through teaching, through visions, through his Word, and often through the Holy Spirit impressing something upon our hearts.

The most important thing to do is seeking to identify God's voice in the midst of all the other voices you may be hearing, including friends, family, church, etc. Remember, too, his voice will always be in line with the Word of God. What is he trying to say to you?

Quite possibly, however, there might not be anything specific, so don't make things more uncomfortable for yourself by trying to assign to God a purpose that's not really there. Difficulties can be just the normal groanings of a creation held in suspension, until Christ's perfect healing comes at his 2nd coming. Distinguishing between the two is where wisdom must enter.

"Oh No, Not Again!"
How To Deal With Repetitive Sins

Sometimes our *reservoir* of godly intention is just *too low* to resist temptation, and we bite into it again and again. It's rather like pressing one's thumb on a leaky faucet. No matter how slow the leak, we just can't stop the flow…the pressure builds and builds, eventually jetting out from beneath our thumb. And, once again, we make a choice to sin. Our spiritual, physical or emotional "lure" has been so well embedded into our psyche that we can't seem to look away. Perhaps our passions are too enflamed from previously inappropriate thought patterns, either by childhood or adulthood indiscretions. Like a bad tooth infection, habit has enrooted itself, and we lack enough spiritual resolve or godly conviction to win over it. So, we just bite into that sin – gambling, porn, alcohol, stealing, credit card abuse, gluttony, etc. - again and again. Our spiritual sensitivities have been dulled to the point that we are unable to exert significant control over our evil impulses. A particular sin has now become uncomfortably repetitive, and our "hair trigger" fires off a sinful attitude or action without much struggle at all. How can we successfully overcome these things?

First, Repent From Your Heart.

Be honest here. As much as possible, regard your sin with deep disrespect and honor the Lord with a heart of genuine repentance. Recognize your loss of control over things and reach out wholeheartedly for God's mercy, grace and restoration. Humble yourselves greatly and receive his forgiveness. Bathe yourself in Scriptural truth, and he will cleanse you with renewed conviction. Always remember, genuine sorrow moves the heart of God.

>"My sacrifice, O God, is a broken spirit; a broken and contrite heart you, God, will not despise." (Psalm 51:17)

Second, Remove Yourself From Temptation

Distance yourself from any presence or place of temptation (as possible). <u>This means any of the following that apply</u>:

- Completely avoid those TV programs, music, literature, entertainments or anything else that brings you down. These only impassion your *sinful* perspectives to rule your life.
- Consistently avoid places or people that put you in contact with the stuff of your particular habit or addiction.
- Refuse to have close relationship with anyone whose lifestyle tempts or weakens you.
- Be decisive in your daily walk! Don't linger or vacillate, when facing a temptation. Move quickly, or you'll fail once again.

Third, Rebuild Your Infrastructure

At some point, you've got to regain the control over your inner person, both mentally and volitionally. But, you say, *"Ed, that's my problem. How can I resist my sinful impulses?"*

First, regaining spiritual strength, stability and stamina necessitates restoring one's *fundamental* conviction to Jesus Christ. More is needed, of course, but we must start here. Without this key principle being implemented at the heart level, one's spiritual walls will repeatedly crumble. Again, this is because our **desire** to resist sin dissipates greatly, if our faith is left unsecured. Only when the pain and disruption of one's life is significant enough to restore one's love for God will he or she have mastery over their inner person. This uncomfortable process of re-consecrating ourselves to our core conviction of faith goes on and on, making us stronger and more secure by God's grace. Remember, faith is the foundation upon which everything rests. Ephesians 6:16 says:

> "In addition to all this, take up the shield of faith, with which you can extinguish all the flaming arrows of the evil one."

Next, you must re-establish a deeper desire and determination to follow God's will...but this can be difficult after a season of sin, right? Regardless, God is looking at your heart and asking you *even again,* "Do you really love me - *this time?*" Remember, you've worked hard to fall to whatever level of repetitive sin in which you find yourself! God will no doubt require you to work *just* as hard in order to **purify** and **re-patriot** yourself to the things of Christ. Jeremiah says:

> "The heart is more deceitful than all else and is desperately sick; Who can understand it? I the Lord, search the heart, I test the mind, Even to give to each man according to his ways." (17:9,10)

Peter responded three times in commitment to the three times he denied the Lord. That continuity may not be God's plan for everyone, but it says something important in God's mind about the need for some sort of restorative process after a period of rebellion. Your infrastructure has been compromised and weakened, and it will most likely take an equally significant season of time to restore it.

> "Therefore, strengthen your feeble arms and weak knees. Make level paths for your feet, so that the lame may not be disabled, but rather healed." (Hebrews 12:12, 13)

The "secret" of success here is to restore consistency to our perspective-passion-purpose responses within us that have broken down through repetitive sins. Think of it like putting logs on a fire out in the woods. Let's say that you've got two mental fires going - one we'll call evil thinking and the other, godly thinking. In preparation for the dark, cold nights of temptation ahead, gather together as many mental logs you can find. *These should be godly truths with spiritual passions tied to them.* They may be catchy points of wisdom, doctrinal or practical truths, special hymns or scriptures that have strong inner meaning to you, and, therefore, inspire *heart felt conviction*. When you face those same old debilitating urges at the onset of temptation, grab onto an impassioned log of truth and throw it onto the fire of your thinking! You may need to throw your *biggest* logs onto the "godly fire" at first, but you'll get the hang of it after a while, with God's help. The more impassioned, super-charged and Scripturally-focused truths you put on the Godly fire, the hotter it gets. Over time, the *ungodly* fire will die down, due to lack of fuel. Your inner person will grow increasingly more sensitive, strong and stable in your spiritual life race.

Again, this implies learning to not travel down the road of fearful, lustful and other inadvisable thoughts. But, even more, it's acquiring a deeply held set of spiritual perspectives and principles of living that you hold on to in times of temptation. And, you only get them from seeking God diligently in his Word. You've heard about wearing out your knees regarding prayer? How about wearing out your thumbs as you search through the pages of God's Truth! That's what it's going to take, if you're serious about breaking the chains of habit.

> *"How can a young man keep his way pure? By living according to your word...I have hidden your word in my heart that I might not sin against you."* (Ps. 119:9, 11)

Together, let's model the spiritual maturity and running stamina that the Apostle Paul found in his relationship with God as our goal:

> *"... whatever was to my profit I now consider loss for the sake of Christ...I consider everything a loss compared to the surpassing greatness of knowing Christ Jesus my Lord..."* (Phil. 3:7, 8)

Fourth, <u>Re-Apply</u> Spiritual Principles

All of us have had sins that cling to our spiritual feet. We usually attack them in heart-wrenching prayers such as, "Jesus, deliver me, *please* deliver me...and change me within."

Although that's definitely part of the process, at some point we must also move from prayer alone...to principle. In other words, we've got to **apply critical actions** in order to overcome the sin that "so easily entangles..." (Heb. 12:1). Yes, this always includes continuing to pray, of course, but "magic-like" petitions ("Lord, change me!") must move toward more mature petitions, such as:

- *"Lord, help me be more faithful in seeking fellowship opportunities, especially this week at the men's study group."*
  ...instead of "Lord, give me strength. I just don't feel like going to Bible Study tonight."
- *"Lord, forgive me for toying with sin in my thoughts. Help me to focus upon these powerful verses I've just discovered."*
  ...instead of "Lord, remove those sinful thoughts from me."

Spiritual strength and stamina come from exercising God's principles of spiritual living. Growth isn't just a prayer away, ***it's a process away***. It comes by way of disciplining ourselves to faithfully apply Scriptural principles of attitude and action with consistency...with the indwelling enablement of God's Holy Spirit.

During the rebuilding process, however, remember that God knows what's going on, even when you or I don't. The struggle is part of the rebuilding process, but God will restore us, as we begin to more consistently *implement* the things he's asking of us. And, if we're sidelined for a while, let's just be patient and not push too hard, even when we want to jump back into teaching or serving others. Let's wait for God's restorative process within us to evidence itself with consistency before jumping ahead of him and diving into intensive ministry.

Above all, let's *learn* from God what we're supposed to learn. Along the way, always avoid playing the blame game, for God is never responsible for our improper choices or difficulties. Remember, too, that time can be a great healer.

Your Spiritual Tool Box

Today's Project:
Refusing Repetitive Sin

Your Blueprint:
*"In your struggle against sin you have not yet resisted to the point of shedding your blood. And have you forgotten the exhortation that addresses you as sons?
'My son, do not regard lightly the discipline of the Lord, nor be weary when reproved by him.
For the Lord disciplines the one he loves, and chastises every son whom he receives.'"*
(Heb. 12:5,6)

Keeping It Plumb:

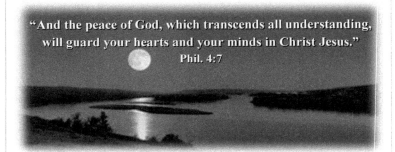

"And the peace of God, which transcends all understanding, will guard your hearts and your minds in Christ Jesus."
Phil. 4:7

Everyone sins, and all of us will experience spiritually good days and spiritually bad ones, too. The wisdom in these verses is that we should have a "middle of the road" feeling about our failures. We should not be **cavalier** about them nor unnecessarily **casual** about the discipline that God may use in our lives to turn us from sin. On the other hand, neither should we feel so guilty over repetitious sins that we lose hope and fall into a shame filled outlook about life. The peace of God as a result of a life lived in discipline and purity is like a river flowing gently through the soul.

"Are You A Long or Short Distance Runner?"

I've never enjoyed running as an exercise, but from my 40's forward, I got into it to keep my weight down. It worked really well until I reached a point where my joints seemed to be adversely affected, so I started biking instead of running as my primary exercise.

When I did run, however, I found myself going only 2 to 3 miles a day. So, you'd have to call me a short distance runner. But, I have a friend by the name of Rob, who travels around the country to participate in 26-mile marathons. He's really into it, having expensive running shoes, distance indicators, and running gear. And, he normally runs in the neighborhood of 12 miles a day just to stay in shape for the big races. Quite a neighborhood!

In the animal world, humans are vastly *inferior* regarding speed. For instance, Cheetahs can attain short bursts of speed well over 62 mph, the American quarter horse has topped 55 mph, and greyhounds can reach 43 mph. The human sprinting record of 27.8 mph was set by Usain Bolt during the final 100 meter sprint at the World Championships event in Berlin on August 16th, 2009.

In the spiritual realm, we also find that some are sprinters and some are distance runners. Our races, of course, do vary in type and duration, but they bring to us the challenge of staying pure under temptation, patient while waiting for answers to prayer, resilient in faith while facing ongoing difficulties, etc.. Now, some believers are spiritually strong in short times of challenge, but tend to break down or drop out of the race when longer times of trial and temptation occur. Others, however, are models of patient endurance, staying in the spiritual race no matter how long or difficult the challenge.

Short distance runners are not what Christ wants us to be, for many can sprint through short seasons of challenge, but not so many have the spiritual stamina to endure a marathon temptation. Biblically speaking, Joseph and Daniel are two long distance runners, whose stories of patience and courage stand out in the pages of Scripture. The Apostle Peter, on the other hand, seems to be a personality defined by shorter bursts of commitment, along with John Mark and Thomas. Here's a formula for becoming a long-distance runner for Christ.

Desire + Determination + Discipline => Distance

Long distance runners have <u>Desire</u>. In other words, they're motivated deeply enough to stay in the race regardless of the circumstances. It's actually about the way they think, which gives them a strong inner "want," allowing them to "faith it through to the end." Their spiritual desire to serve Christ and to be used by him is deeply embedded into their soul. Like Paul, they would say…

> "I want to know Christ—yes, to know the power of his resurrection and participation in his sufferings, becoming like him in his death, and so, somehow, attaining to the resurrection from the dead. Not that I have already obtained all this, or have already arrived at my goal, but I press on to take hold of that for which Christ Jesus took hold of me. Brothers and sisters, I do not consider myself yet to have taken hold of it. But one thing I do: Forgetting what is behind and straining toward what is ahead, I press on toward the goal to win the prize for which God has called me heavenward in Christ Jesus." (Phil. 3:10-14)

Paul states his desire quite plainly, "to know his power and become like him." Paul met Jesus on the road to Damascus, and he met him again, I believe, when he was shown the "3rd heaven." He also talks about other visions he had the privilege to experience as well, so his personal acquaintance with Jesus, though different from the other disciples, was intensely powerful in shaping his spiritual motivations over the years.

If we've come to know Christ as Savior, there still remains the larger part of knowing him as a person, which can only be filled by walking a daily and intimate path with him through prayer and Bible study. By listening to him in the Word and responding to him by prayer, we define and deepen our relationship with him. In this way, our desire to know more of him is never quenched, and we retain a spiritual thirst that drives us forward in obedience and service.

Long distance runners have <u>Determination</u>. If the desire is strong, so will be the outworking of that desire…a determined effort to attain a goal or achieve a result. For Paul's part, he is not concerned as much about his failures and inadequacies, but *"strains forward"* for the prize. A runner in these Grecian games might have received a garland of olive, laurel or pine, but Paul's prize was his reward in heaven. This desire was so motivating to him, it gave him unparalleled commitment to attain it…a rigorous determination to be all he could be for Jesus, his magnificent Savior and Lord. And, his vision never diminished.

If you're having trouble staying the course and/or defeating a particularly nasty sin in your life, I would suggest that you reconsider the prize of your spiritual race. How much does heaven mean to you? How much do the words, "Well done, good and faithful servant," mean to you? How great and how pleasurable will be the eternal joys and rewards we receive from our Lord, when heaven bids us come home? Surely, all our sensual and earthly difficulties demonstratively shrink before the glorious beauty of heaven's gates! The old hymn says it well.

> Turn your eyes upon Jesus
> Look full in His wonderful face
> And the things of earth will grow strangely dim
> In the light of His glory and grace
> (Helen H. Lemmel)

Long distance runners have <u>Discipline</u>. Because of the long-distance runner's deep desire and his enduring determination, what follows is an deep capacity for self-discipline. Such a runner's practice schedule is filled and without gaps. He or she employs a wide range of disciplined activities, muscle strengthening work outs and diet constraints for acquiring distance capability.

Spirituality is no different. Distance-running discipleship requires unique dedication to the principles of Christian living, despite any desires to the contrary. That's why sensually driven personalities don't measure up for long distance endurance in the things of God. Yes, these folks are saved, of course, but the process of *sanctification* is often slow and bumpy for them, because of the attractiveness of sin and/or the nagging need to pull away from the temptations inherent in their daily races.

So, who are you in this discussion? Is your spiritual life more characterized as that of a sprinter or is it similar to a distance runner? There's still plenty of time to learn the *fundamentals* of distance running, so step out and embrace your future by...

"Forgetting what is behind and straining toward what is ahead,
...press on toward the goal to win the prize for which
God has called me heavenward in Christ Jesus."

Your Spiritual Tool Box

Today's Project:
Running In The Spirit

Your Blueprint:
"Therefore, since we are surrounded by such a great cloud of witnesses, let us throw off everything that hinders and the sin that so easily entangles. And let us run with perseverance the race marked out for us, fixing our eyes on Jesus, the pioneer and perfecter of faith." (Hebrews 12:1, 2)

Keeping It Plumb:
Long or short distance runners need to keep focused on the race. For believers, this means keeping our eyes on our coach, the Lord Jesus Christ. So, if you want more stamina in your running, invite him into every aspect of your daily life. Then, amidst all the stresses and challenges of life, you'll find yourself blessed in all you do. Otherwise, you'll experience needless wandering and unwanted difficulties. Seek God and his will faithfully in all you do, for *"seeking builds stamina!"*

Praying For...
✓ Dad's healing
✓ Pastor's preaching
✓ Leadership retreat
✓ Good Health
✓ A new car

My ~~Prayer~~ Wish List?

"Ed, you called it a wish list, but it should read, prayer list, right?"

Actually, I changed it to "wish list," to point out that too many folks mistakenly confuse the two. Yes, we are seeking blessing and provision from the hand of God, and that's great...he really does want to provide for our needs. The problem occurs, however, when we begin to confuse needs with wants. Then, our prayer list can easily turn into a wish list with high expectations for "presents" from God...sort of an ongoing spiritual Christmas! Let's talk about it.

We should begin by defining prayer. Prayer is simply communicating with God, whether it's asking him for something or praising him for his blessing in our lives. Like any relationship, communication is a *fundamental* component involved in bringing two people together. In a relationship with God, prayer is our part of the relationship, where we talk with him, while reading the Bible is mostly God's part, because it's there that he talks with us. And, like any relationship, learning how to say things properly and listen intently is important, even when talking with God.

A little boy was kneeling beside his bed next to his mother and grandmother, softly saying his prayers. He really loved his gramma, because she was always so kind and giving, especially at Christmas time.

"Dear God, please bless Mommy...and Daddy...and please give me a good night's sleep." Suddenly he looked up and *shouted, "And don't forget to give me a bicycle for my birthday!"*

"There is no need to shout like that," said his mother. "God isn't deaf."

"No," said the little boy, *"but Gramma is!"* (jokes.christiansunite.com/Prayer/Speak_Up.shtml)

I think many Christians believe, erroneously, that if we shout out our wish list to God, he may hear us a bit better. The truth is, of course, that he already knows what we both need and want for birthdays, Christmas or at any other day of the year. The *fundamental* truth about God is that he is both eternally omniscient and providential…nothing takes him by surprise nor dissuades him from fulfilling his purposeful will in our lives. Okay, then why do we pray?

First, we pray because he tells us to. That's a fundamental truth about Christian living. All of us need to simply acknowledge and obey, even when it seems pointless or fruitless, even though nothing seems to be happening. The truth is that God is continually working behind the scenes to accomplish his will, whether we see it or not.

Secondly, we pray because communication is the "stuff" of relationships, even with God. Through constant prayer and Bible reading, we learn about God, about ourselves and about how to both relate to God and manage our expectations of relationship with him.

Thirdly, however, we also pray because our sovereign God *allows himself to be moved by the petitions of his people.* He wants to hear our joys, our sorrows, our expectations, and our requests, but he responds to us in accordance (or in line with) his will for our lives. The awesome part of it all, though, is that God in his sovereignty is capable of including into his perfect plan the very words and concerns that we pray about *before we actually pray about them!*

> *"And when you pray, do not keep on babbling like pagans, for they think they will be heard because of their many words. Do not be like them, for your Father knows what you need before you ask him."* (Matt. 6:7,8)

Such knowledge is beyond our understanding, of course. Nevertheless, we should pray and do everything God asks of us in spite of the fact that we do not completely understand it or its ramifications. I spent three years at Seminary trying to "unscrew the inscrutable," as Chuck Swindoll likes to say. But, in the end, any professor, pastor or pew-sitter like myself can only scratch the surface of the attributes of Almighty God. But, the implication of all this is that we shouldn't be praying to **change** the will of God…ever. We pray to **find** the will of God and to worship him for his magnificent glory and matchless lovingkindness.

So, What's On Your Prayer List?

Now, back to the question of what we *should* put on our PRAYER list. Again, we should be looking at praying less for wants and wishes and more for needs and God's will. Here's an example.

I just slipped out of my office and went down to put a load of laundry into the washing machine. About an hour ago, I put some "pre-wash" on a couple of grease spots I got on my shorts last night from popcorn at a baseball game. But, when I started to put them into the washing machine, I noticed that the pre-washing solution had greatly discolored the material, which I had let dry (instead of soaking).

Now, I can pray that God will "magically or miraculously" restore the discolored spots in my shorts, which he certainly could do. But, mature praying isn't like that, for God isn't a heavenly eraser, who exists to simply wash away every mistake we make in life. Instead, godly praying simply acknowledges a mistake and seeks God's help to do better next time.

Nor is God a spiritual Santa, holding us in his lap while we review with him all the things we'd like to receive. For instance, we pray for the money to get a new car, and, unfortunately, we fall short on the funds to buy it. So, we get disappointed and discouraged by our perception that God didn't care enough. Or, perhaps we're told that our faith wasn't adequate for him to bless us, when in reality it had little to do with our faith. Believing in his innate ability to bless us is powerful, but believing that he will always give us what we by faith ask for...that's **presumption.** We should never presumptively ask God for anything. We can pray for that new car, of course, but we must ask God for it only as it *falls in line with his will.* Jesus instructs us to pray, *"Thy will be done, on earth as it is in heaven."*

I, frankly, don't want to get anything IF it's not within God's purposeful will for myself and my family. Are you kidding? If I got *everything* I've prayed for over the years, I know I would have gotten into deep trouble. Think about it. You pray for that big-paycheck job and don't get it. Then, two months later, you read that the company had an explosion, which destroyed the business for ever. Or, you pray for that more expensive home, even increasing your payment unwisely by 26%. At first, you were mad at God for not "hearing your prayer," only to find out that your spouse loses his/her job six months later...and it would have bankrupted you. No...I ONLY want what GOD wants when praying, for I gave up being "master designer of the universe" years ago and find great peace in that conviction.

> *"Now listen, you who say, "Today or tomorrow we will go to this or that city, spend a year there, carry on business and make money." Why, you do not even know what will happen tomorrow. What is your life? You are a mist that appears for a little while and then vanishes. Instead, you ought to say, "If it is the Lord's will, we will live and do this or that."* James 4:13-15

Keep in mind that there are times when we might actually know whether it is God's will or not God's will...perhaps when praying for things like our spiritual growth or becoming more forgiving or loving toward others, for instance. Or, on occasion, we can pray with assurance, because the need seems so obvious and so great for an act of compassion (e.g. hurricane victims, justice for a horrific crime, etc.) or for in support of a particular ministry in need. The Apostle John says in this regard:

> *"This is the confidence we have in approaching God: that if we ask anything according to his will, he hears us. And if we know that he hears us—whatever we ask—we know that we have what we asked of him."*
> (I John 5:14, 15)

So, prayer is both fundamentally simple and extremely important at the same time. Pray that it becomes all that it should be in your list of spiritual responsibilities.

Your Spiritual Tool Box

Today's Project:
Praying In The Spirit

Your Blueprint:
"And pray in the Spirit on all occasions with all kinds of prayers and requests. With this in mind, be alert and always keep on praying for all the Lord's people."
(Eph. 6:18)

Keeping It Plumb:
The above is sort of an odd way of saying it, but I think the Apostle Paul is telling us to pray in an attitude of obedient faith. Faith is a given, of course, for step one is to believe that one's prayers are being heard in the first place. But, additionally, I think that we must also have a willing, submissive and yielded spirit on our part. Then God, who abides in us, will listen to our obedient hearts as we seek his blessing for ourselves and for our friends in Christ.

Stop! You must not offend anyone, anytime, in any way, for any reason. This is America!

Living In A PC World

"The avoidance...of forms of expression or action that are perceived to exclude, marginalize, or insult groups of people who are socially disadvantaged or discriminated against."
(https://www.bing.com/search?q=political+correctness&form)

"That's not politically correct!" shouts out a media personality to another more conservative member on the panel.

"There's no such thing as political correctness!" returns the accused panel member on the TV show, "Ground Zero: The Search For Truth."

And, for the next half hour a philosophical battle emerges over how people should accept one another's differences. The liberal panel members think that we live in an emerging culture of inclusive acceptance, tolerance and support. The conservative members of the media panel believe that culture has definite standards, which may rightfully reject certain types of behaviors. On and on it goes until the discussion leader ends the program.

"Okay, well, it's been a lively discussion. Thanks to everyone for your opinions and helpful points of view. And, to you who are watching...you have a great day. See you next week on, "Ground Zero: The Search For Truth."

This little vignette is a typical media scenario. When it's all finished, little has been settled and the people watching either walk away with the same opinion they had at the beginning or just remain confused as ever. That's because "truth" isn't an opinion, it's a reality. The problem with the "world's" type of truth is that it doesn't recognize the reality of ground zero (God's truth).

As believers, however, we sometimes get angry, when listening to such "gobbly-goop," knowing that God's revelation in the Scriptures *is* true and reliable, which categorically means that some things are wrong (offensive or not) and that other things are good and right. But, we must also be forthright in acknowledging that even Christians have differing opinions regarding doctrine and Biblical values at times. That's because we are fallible, even though the Bible is not. It is inspired ("God breathed") by the Spirit of God and is fundamentally sound in both precept and principle. Paul talks to Timothy about this, as well as to you and I, in his letter to Timothy:

> *"All Scripture is God-breathed and is useful for teaching, rebuking, correcting and training in righteousness…"* (II Timothy 2:15)

And, the Apostle Peter also reiterates this in his letter to the churches.

> *"Above all, you must understand that no prophecy of Scripture came about by the prophet's own interpretation of things. For prophecy never had its origin in the human will, but prophets, though human, spoke from God as they were carried along by the holy Spirit."* (II Peter 1:20-21)

Okay, we understand that we have the Truth of God revealed to us in person by God's Son, Jesus, which has also been written down for us in the Bible. But, we also realize that the world of non-believers does not accept this reality, and in fact has come to a point where, "The truth is…THERE IS NO TRUTH!" Yes, as we've noted before, this is logical nonsense, but nevertheless be aware that the world has created this *inclusive* soup for people like you and I to adopt.

Actually, this "inclusive" thinking began in the Clinton White House years as a way to deal with the emerging clash between conservatism and liberalism. It sought to avoid "offending" people who had differing political viewpoints, but realistically had Christian beliefs in its cross hairs. A better title would be, "Moral Vacillation," because it's essential focus was to eliminate anything coming close to Biblical Truth, absolute truth, or sound and repeatable standards to which people and cultures should adhere. But, the Gospel is rarely "inclusive," and as such, it will always offend some folks who won't accept it or the moral values it espouses. That's okay, for we are fundamentally called to proclaim *God's Truth*, not *man's wishes* for some sort of moral diversity, unhealthy tolerance, wayward multi-culturalism or other inclusive philosophies.

However, we *can agree* on some issues from a Christian perspective. **First,** showing kindness in the face of diverse thinking, opposing opinions and cultural differences *is a must.* Christ wants us to be loving and kind enough such that God's truth...no matter how antagonistic it is to a someone else...will hopefully be received by the positive way it is presented. In the long run, of course, God is not overly concerned about "offending" someone's opinions, but we should still model Paul's admonition to be *"speaking the truth in love."* (Ephesians 4:15)

Secondly, we should be willing and ready to make a defense of the Gospel, as Peter reminds us in his first letter, chapter three, verses 15-16:

> *'But in your hearts revere Christ as Lord. Always be prepared to give an answer to everyone who asks you to give the reason for the hope that you have. But do this with gentleness and respect, keeping a clear conscience, so that those who speak maliciously against your good behavior in Christ may be ashamed of their slander."*

Notice that Christ is our Lord, not a self-serving, liberal philosophy. To me this means that we have a responsibility to "push back" against those that would marginalize or denounce Christian faith and values in the public arena. Indeed, we should be "prepared" to give reasonable answers...well-thought out and verbalized answers...to those who either opposes us or are sincerely seeking the truth. Ask yourself, "How equipped am I right now to answer everyday questions about my faith...its roots, its doctrines, its moral precepts and principles, even the hard to answer issues that are sometimes raised by unbelievers? Am I a reliable witness for the things of Christ?"

Lastly, are you willing to share these things with another person with gentleness and respect, along with a good conscience. I remember a guy who owned a Christian bookstore in Connecticut, where I was raised. When anyone visited his stored he'd be sure to come over and start asked questions. He saw it, I guess, as an evangelistic thing, but he would always get into topics that focused on opinions, and, of course, his answers were always right. People got offended, not by the truth of God, but by the rudeness and lack of grace that he demonstrated. In my mind, he probably hurt a lot more people than he ever helped.

Also, a word of advice about taking on the PC crowd. If our conscience reminds us of recent sins in attitude or action, it's probably best that we keep our mouth shut before entering into doctrinal discussions or handling PC issues with non-believers. Guilt tends to dull our insights and erode spiritual logic. Others can zero in rather quickly on our weaknesses, doubts and lack of spiritual confidence. Better to stay quietly safe on the sidelines rather than trying to win battles when you're already seriously wounded.

Your Spiritual Tool Box

Today's Project:
Culture Verses Christ

Your Blueprint:
"If it is possible, **as far as it depends on you,**
live at peace with everyone.."
(Romans 12:18)

Keeping It Plumb:

It seems like the verse above would be easily followed. But, in 21st century America and beyond, it is certainly not a slam-dunk! There are so many captivated people out there, yes, captivated folks who are caught in the net of "nice thinking." Political correctness is nice thinking, because it doesn't want to offend anyone and avoids this by *accepting* most everything and everyone, regardless of their moral viewpoints. I would agree that we must always respond with kindness and patience, which is how the Bible says we should act. But, with individual attitudes and behaviors that "offend" the Bible's teaching, we have to disagree…sometimes strongly…in order to speak up for God and his will. Culture is always liquid, moving and changing like waves creeping in and out upon a beach. Christ's teachings, however, never ebb and flow with the moral tides.

Fantasy Verses Reality

Vacations are fun!

You may like going to Universal Studios, Dolly World, Sea World or some other well-known resort to "get away from it all," but my wife and I enjoy going to Disney World each year. We enjoy all the rides and especially the Disney hotels, our favorite being the Port Orleans Riverside. The setting is the Southern countryside, with a laid-back atmosphere amidst moss covered oaks and winding rivers.

Whatever your choice getaway is, keep in mind that what happens on vacation or in your fantasy world isn't real, lasting or often true-to-life. In fact, trying to live in a fantasy world is the definition of insanity! But, so many folks…even in the church at times…live on the level of just imagination, fun and games. So, whether you're reading a good book while sailing to the Bahamas or sliding down a snow-covered slope near Jackson Hole Wyoming, it's mostly just temporary frivolity.

I remember way back in high school, when one of my teachers referred to Walt Disney as espousing an "unnecessary escape from the real world." Now, Disney World is great, but all the enjoyable rides, the song-filled shows, the beautifully secluded resort grounds…everything…is not real life, for sure. Most people understand this, recognizing that it's just a relaxing, temporary escape folks enjoy and call it a *vacation*. The "magic" of any vacation, whether on a cruise ship, sitting on the beach in Acapulco, or visiting the Grand Canyon, is that it gets us away from incessant stress of the daily grind. But, let's look at some other, not-so-good, *spiritual* vacations that some believers unwisely take *all year round*.

Visiting MATERIALISM METROPOLIS

Here's the sad thing. Too many believers are spending lots of money and too much time and energy accumulating huge homes, automobiles, clothes, boats and other nice but unnecessary toys. Things aren't evil, but when the accumulation of them garners so much of our time and energy, then our personal relationship with Christ, our family relationships and our fellowship responsibilities can suffer greatly for it. I've seen so many marriages broken up by unnecessary materialism and debt which could have been avoided if the acquisition of "things" was more wisely handled. Certainly, a Mercedes doesn't bring on a divorce or a upper middle class home in suburbia doesn't cause a family to disintegrate into distant and self-absorbed relationships. But, the path to acquiring such things must be followed very carefully to avoid such traps, along with God's wise counsel along the way. God does bring riches to some and uses the wealth of godly individuals to support wonderful ministries...granted   But, that's no excuse for believing that you or I *must have* or are *entitled* to such things.

As believers, we have everything to live for...God's blessing here on earth and a glorious home in heaven awaiting us after our earthly departure. Wealthy or not, on this side of heaven God promises to provide for all our material needs, and he never lies. There may be a Chevrolet in the garage instead of a Cadillac or a hamburger on the grill instead of a steak, but God's grace will always meet our needs as long as we are living according to his will.

> *"And we know that in all things God works for the good of those who love him, who have been called according to his purpose."* (Rom 8:28)

> "And my God will meet all your needs according to the riches of his glory in Christ Jesus." (Phil. 4:19)

All of our future needs will be provided for as well, for the Lord Jesus is in heaven preparing a dwelling place especially for us:

> "And if I go and prepare a place for you, I will come back and take you to be with me that you also may be where I am." (John 14:13)

Travelling To "LA LA LAND"

This one's hard to face, but it is absolutely true: You and I will have issues, temptations, difficulties, stresses, struggles, hardships and failure in our Christian life experience. Jesus himself said, *""I have told you these things, so that in me you may have peace. In this world you will have trouble. But take heart! I have overcome the world."* (John 16:33)

Notice that the peace of Christ is not found in the absence of trouble or in fun-filled vacations, but in the midst of life's challenges. Too many believers think that being a believer means that no one will sue them falsely, no one will T-bone their car, no family member will get seriously sick, no investment will "go south," no temptation will overwhelm them on occasion, and...well, you get the idea.

There was a fellow college student that developed a brain tumor in only a few weeks, which took his life. He was a model Christian in his walk and was very well respected on campus. Still, God took him home "early." I have a good friend, who was a great golfing buddy. In fact, he was an area champion...semi-pro. He called me on a Sunday night, saying he had to cancel Monday's game, because he thought he was coming down with the flu. Unfortunately, he had a urinary track infection that quickly spread, closed down all his organs by Wednesday and took his life on Thursday. I also know a believer who had to bankrupt his business due to lack of enough new customers, and I also know a well-known Pastor, whose wife left him for a woman. Three of my closest friends had sons who got caught in the drug culture, and they prayed fervently for a season of time for God to free their teenage sons from its grasp and for the grace to survive the stress from it all in the meantime (all three teenagers are walking with the Lord today, praise God!). There's just no spiritual "La La Land" out there where believers float around on a pre-heaven pillow of uninterrupted peace and quiet. But, in the midst of all of the "issues" that any of us may face, the Lord Jesus promises to be with us with his grace and guidance.

Staying At ENTERTAINMENT RESORT

One of the most recognizable, yet the stealthiest fantasy problems today, come from the entertainment world. What Communism stated as its objective in the 60's (destroy America from within), media moguls and writers are accomplishing with avaricious delight today, and that is the disintegration of the inner moral fiber of the American public. From a spiritual point of view, the electronic age has brought with it all the tools that Satan and his host needs to feed the nature of man with false narratives, corrupt imaginations and dysfunctional realities.

For example, at one time "Father Knows Best" was a top television show, basing its creative plots around having good relationships, respect for society and authority, and honorable lifestyles. Now, one of the top shows is Family Guy, going into its 15th season and full of bathroom and sexual gags, gay and transsexual agendas, political satire, moral diversity, and cultural carnality. It essentially laughs at everything that is morally and culturally sound, while sending a few self-serving barbs at obvious and genuine evils such as racism and materialism.

> The Parents Television Council (PTC), a conservative, non-profit watchdog, has attacked the series since its premiere and has branded various episodes as "Worst TV Show of the Week" [and] has placed the show on their annual lists of "Worst Prime-Time Shows for Family Viewing...." The Federal Communications Commission has received multiple petitions requesting that the show be blocked from broadcasting on indecency grounds. Tucker and the PTC have both accused the show of portraying religion negatively, and of being racist.
> (https://en.wikipedia.org/wiki/Family_Guy)

This is just one show of many, without even discussing movies, Broadway shows, internet, newspapers, magazines and literature. But, I'm not just talking about entertainment that is evil in its content or intent. The whole experience of imbibing fantasy plots of science fiction in full digital detail and creative alternative realities, for instance, has the subtle effect of dulling one's focus upon the genuine reality God and of his Son, Jesus. After all, how can salvation rise to the excitement of another voyage into the unknown with the crew of the Enterprise or partnering with Han Solo as he streaks through the galaxies in the Millennium Falcon? Perhaps the world of NCIS captivates your imagination and you enjoy these crime investigators as they uncover the truth of another navy murder? Maybe your kids are into Harry Potter and all the mind-captivating shenanigans of three young disciples in the world of magic?

However, the real issue with all this entertainment is not that there is necessarily any evil intent involved (though there can be and often is). The danger, however, lies in what I call "spiritual de-sensitization." This whole fantasy imaging we call entertainment is NOT REAL...it's just an imaginative cultural and technical phenomenon. It enables people to indulge their emotional pleasures, watching 30 television fantasies or, for $12 a pop, a *full-length fantasy* in surround sound at the local movie theater. But, the plots, the words, the characters, the exploits...*all of this is made up, right?*

We all understand this, of course. But, when all this fantasy is indulged in repeatedly, a foggy, lethargic, and de-sensitized spirituality *can* easily overcome both non-believer and believer. Again, without really recognizing it, we become *drugged with indifference* to the realities of God, Jesus Christ, Biblical Truth and spiritual responsibility. Yes, it's not true of everyone, and, yes, it takes time, and, yes, not everyone can be seriously harmed by it all. BUT...it happens, and it can hurt any of us, if we are not careful to put restraints upon this subtly coercive culture of fantasy that surrounds us. And, it definitely has detrimental effects upon our young people.

In summary, I'm not suggesting that you never go to seek the next Star Trek movie or that you should immediately throw out your TV, or that you should burn all your books of fiction unless Christian focused. But, let me suggest two Scriptural principles that can be applied individually by all of us in order to avoid Entertainment Ally dangers. Choosing either one and applying it appropriately, might be a good choice for many to make, if they remain open to God's direction.

First Choice Do not **over-indulge yourself** even in "good" programming, if it tends to produce within you an *overwhelming* amount of fantasy fun. If you begin to sense any unnecessary spiritual encroachment and/or desensitization, pray for the Spirit's wisdom, search the pages of Scripture for God's truth, and then seriously consider cutting away some of the fantasy clutter. In other words, be willing to avoid that which is *okay* for no other reason than you genuinely want *more* of that which is *better.*

Second Choice Be willing to take the more drastic remedy for spiritual survival, if God is telling YOU to do so. In *this* case, be ready to **completely eliminate** specific forms of entertainment programming (e.g. specific programs or even the source...television, movies, internet, etc.) for the love of Jesus Christ and God's will for your life. Remember, you're not doing it because it's necessarily evil, just that you see a strong, spiritual hindrance in it that God's wants you personally to avoid. Do it without shame, regardless of what others may think or say. Remember, you don't have to convince others of anything, but you do have to please your Lord and Savior, who holds our REAL future in his hand. So, remember this, too: *"...if your right hand causes you to stumble, cut it off and throw it away. It is better for you to lose one part of your body than for your whole body to go into hell."* (Matt. 5:30)

Your Spiritual Tool Box

Today's Project:
Targeting Television

Your Blueprint:
"Finally, brothers and sisters, whatever is true, whatever is noble, whatever is right, whatever is pure, whatever is lovely, whatever is admirable - if anything is excellent or praiseworthy - think about such things."
(Phil. 4:8)

Keeping It Plumb:
I don't like for single out something unnecessarily, but television is such an obvious issue to be concerned about in all our lives. For the small part of it that seems to be free of the influence of sinful thinking, there is a superabundance of spiritually antagonistic advertising, pernicious programming and politically slanted news casting. Add to it the addition of satellite and cable programming, and it's no wonder why our culture both in and out of the church is reeling with immorality, rampant violence and worldly thinking. There's just not a lot of wholesome stuff in it one could characterize as being "true...noble ...right...pure...lovely...admirable...excellent...praiseworthy." When it strays from this, let's be quick to turn it off, okay?

Living In The Battle Zone

The other day a thought crossed my mind about how fortunate we are to be living in the United States. It has a protected geographic location, far enough away from the Hitlers, Stalins, Ho Chi Minhs and other world dictators, who have brought carnage, death and physical destruction to so many people and nations. But, in this new century, the emerging leaps in technology has brought these awful realities much closer to our shores such that we may someday be facing a homeland actually under attack.

Spiritually speaking, however, people of all ethnic and national heritages face an ongoing war with the prince of the air and world demigod called Satan. His influence over world leaders doesn't mean that he forgets about you and I. He and his evil host are actively involved in personal, spiritual warfare with men and women around the globe. Some people, particularly non-Christians, don't even acknowledge his sinister influence in our lives, but we believers see it evidenced all around us.

I should mention that this spiritual war is a protracted one, and will last in the world as long as God allows it to exist. There will also be a final, cataclysmic battle the likes of which the world has never seen. Until then, we live in a constant battle zone of spiritual warfare with all of its death and debris.

From Scripture, we know that the war's outcome has *already been decided*. Satan's power was devastated and his efforts to keep all men and women from spending eternity with God has been eliminated through the cross and resurrection of God's Son, Jesus. Though sin has been initially robbed of its ultimate victory, it's remnants and spiritual debris remain until Christ's second coming. This means that all of us will continue to face **daily battles** that sometimes bring extreme difficulties and struggles into our lives So, here's my question: "How are YOU doing in this war? Here's a list of some of these ongoing battles:

- **The battle of sensual temptation:** We want so much to give in and indulge our fleshly natures, which constantly crave inordinate satisfaction. But, the debris of these frequent slips, side trips and stupid choices can be devastating to our spiritual confidence and relationship with Christ. Nasty habits, broken families and church splits can follow, if such battles are not won.
- **The battle of marital and family success:** There are so many responsibilities in trying to keep things together with our spouses and our children. Financial needs, sexual needs, relational needs, financial difficulties, discipline issues, school challenges, etc., are all exacerbated by Satan to bring spiritual failure, family dis-function and ongoing church problems.
- **The battle of death and loss:** Mankind is spiritually dead, living in separation from intimacy with God. But, even though spiritual intimacy has been restored in the believer's life, we still lose people from our lives that we love along the way, and that hurts…it hurts a lot.
- **The battle of doubt and hope:** We have the Word of God always before us, wonderful Pastors and teachers, and such fantastic spiritual tools today (digital commentaries, teaching websites and other online resources, etc.). Yet, there are days for all of us, where our minds needlessly wander and begin doubting our spiritual foundation, perhaps due to unanswerable questions or difficult life struggles.
- **The battle of physical pain/deterioration:** Like it or not, my golf swing is just not as good as it used to be! (Though I do have some prepared excuses). Time and age wear down our bodies and minds, bringing anything from simple discomfort to severe loss of mobility and/or mental acuity.
- **The battle of fear, anxiety and worry:** Uncertainty is always bothersome. But, it can be crippling at times, if left unresolved. It directly attacks our faith, resulting in loss of confidence and courage. It weakens business, hurts relationships and families, and empties ministry from being all it can be.
- **The battle of difficult relationships:** Getting along with everyone is a challenge, because of differing opinions, personalities and backgrounds. But,

it does seem that some people just enjoy hurting others or causing relational grief...in the family, with relatives, at work or church, friends...wherever.

- **The battle over job and financial provision:** This conflict can be truly devastating for a person or family, for putting "food on the table" is a major responsibility of life. That means having a good job and a secure career path, but achieving this is never easy. My grandson graduated from a prestigious law school and his fiancée is soon to become a Pediatrician. The good money they will step into will not cause them to escape the challenges above. Rich or poor, life seems to hit us all with struggles in this area...sooner or later.

Waging A Successful War

First, all of us must realize that the battles will keep coming! Temptations don't stop, needs don't diminish, difficulties won't disappear, and weaknesses continue to bother us, even though we can make some great headway at times. Human nature is rotten at its core, and, along with Satan's occasional influences, each day has its continuing set of challenging circumstances.

Second, simple or significant answers aren't end-all solutions. There are a lot of variables and appropriate principles and precepts to learn for meandering through these waterways successfully. Along the way, God has ordained that in this world, you and I will have trouble (John 14:33) and that means facing inevitable battles.

There is a strategic key, however, which is learning to lean on Christ in the midst of all of it. This is the singular thread of strength, resource, and common spiritual necessity...which we'll call spiritual intimacy.

In real physical warfare it is absolutely critical to maintain communication and supply lines to the front. If this line of assistance deteriorates or fails, the warriors up front are doomed to die, because they will run out of the ammunition, food and the practical support necessary to carry on the war. Spiritual warfare is the same...we need critical resources every day to carry on and win our battles. All of these "battle zones" above require this ongoing resource to sustain and renew our war-torn efforts. Without the Holy Spirit's inner resource, we're also doomed to lose too many battles, needlessly so, simply because we slipped away from the "supply chain" of God's mercy and grace.

So, though it may sound oversimplified, maintaining a close, intimate and consistent relationship with Christ is the critical, common component for success in spiritual warfare. Here is a passage that focuses upon this.

> *"For this reason, I kneel before the Father, from whom every family in heaven and on earth derives its name. I pray that out of his glorious riches he may strengthen you with power through his Spirit in your inner being, so that Christ may dwell in your hearts through faith. And I pray that you, being rooted and established in love, may have power, together with all the Lord's holy people, to grasp how wide and long and high and deep is the love of Christ, and to know this love that surpasses knowledge - that you may be filled to the measure of all the fullness of God. Now to him who is able to do immeasurably more than all we ask or imagine, according to his power that is at work within us, to him be glory in the church and in Christ Jesus throughout all generations, for ever and ever! Amen."* (Ephesians 3:17-21)

Notice, that this passage doesn't say pray for 15 minutes a day, or read two chapters a day in your "through the Bible in a year" program. Neither does it say you must attend the major church services each week and a monthly Bible study. It just says that the Spirit within us is able to empower in our faith, as we are rooted in his Christ's love. Nevertheless, this is the *fundamental* "stuff" of relationship with God. It involves acknowledging him, spending time with him, sharing our issues with him, learning from him, digging into the Word, seeking fellowship and counsel, and being active in personal ministry. So, God's plan for spiritual success is more than *trying to avoid* difficulties or temptations. It's learning to **seek** him in the midst of all those areas of life. Battle Zones are opportunities to seek God's grace and find his perfect will until the spiritual war is finally finished and Christ returns.

So, stay in the battle, *but don't forget your supply line,* okay? You'll be a lonely, unprepared, battle-fatigued and possibly a wounded warrior if you do. There's a better alternative for spiritual soldiering, and it's staying close to our Savior and Lord. He knows the battle zone, and he also has a successful battle plan for everyone, if only they are willing to yield to their commanding officer.

> *"Now to him who is able to do immeasurably more than all we ask or imagine, according to his power that is at work within us, to him be glory in the church and in Christ Jesus throughout all generations, for ever and ever! Amen."*
> (Ephesians 3:20)

Your Spiritual Tool Box

Today's Project:
Know Your Enemy

Your Blueprint:
"Beloved, I urge you as aliens and strangers to abstain from fleshly lusts which wage war against the soul."
(I Peter 2:11)

Keeping It Plumb:

The biggest and most powerful enemy in the arsenal of Satan is the flesh... our appetites, desires and emotions. These are the things that often trip us up, because we crave to be satisfied and appeased in life one way or another. When not satisfied in these areas, we reach outside of the will of God in order to achieve these ends. Instead, learn what triggers Satan uses to draw you into his web of lust, pride, fear and worry, and develop an "early warning system" that shouts out to your inner person, "Okay, here he is again...watch and get ready!" Keep your mental antenna up and looking for those familiar attack zones on the horizon. Always pray and keep alert, "for your enemy prowls around like a hungry lion, looking for someone to devour."

The Honest Truth

    I had a friend call me, who wanted to share something of great interest to him regarding the creation account in Genesis. I agreed, so we met at a coffee place, and he began to share a somewhat controversial way of looking at how the world was created and the time it took for God to bring it all about. I'd seen something like this before, but had forgotten most of it over the years. My friend was a committed and faithful believer, who just wanted to run it by me and see what my thoughts were about it. At the end of our conversation, I expressed my concern over some of the conclusions of this particular view of creation, but I was glad we had the chance to look at it together.

    This experience made me think about how many opinions there are regarding just about everything. My friend represented his thinking well and in an up-front way. Though I somewhat disagreed with his conclusion, I know he has the best of intentions and wasn't trying to trick anybody with some type of theological shenanigans or crazy agenda. But, in today's world, it's frankly very hard to find the truth, wouldn't you agree? Everyone seems bent on expressing their own ideas and many folks just don't have an open mind, if you nicely challenge them. Like someone said, "It's my way or the highway!"

This incident brought up a fundamental problem we have in our culture today...our opinions get in the way of reality and truth! Politics, talk show hosts, college professors, even some pastors...all have their particular slant on things. Advertising moguls promote their opinions probably more so than politicians, for they've got to create gimmicks and catchy jingles to get the attention *and wallets* of potential customers. The product probably doesn't come close to doing what a customer thinks it will, but "who cares, it's another notch on the sales board!" Car salespeople are known as the worst of the bunch and recently were high up on a list of salespeople who customers didn't trust. Life insurance salespeople, financial planners, lawyers, politicians...they all had significant issues in people's minds regarding trust. Even Israel had a huge problem with lying and untruthfulness:

> *"Therefore say to them, 'This is the nation that has not obeyed the LORD its God or responded to correction. Truth has perished; it has vanished from their lips."* (Jer. 7:28)

The worst situations seem to be when people get into discussions about their general views on things. Opinions start flying, even though rarely does anyone know the specifics about anything, or hasn't even met the person being talked about, for instance. Yet, folks jump into the conversation with un-detoured confidence that what they're saying is "absolutely true."

Let's show a bit more humility in these types of conversations, okay. Sharing a viewpoint is a good and responsible thing to do, of course. But, as believers, we know that our words reach the ears of God, so let's not be belligerent or over-opinionated. It creates skepticism in our witness for Christ, if the vessel that presents it is tarnished by pride and ungrounded opinion.

I would suggest sharing most of our viewpoints with, "I believe...." Or, "My thought on that is..." These are gentle ways of sharing opinions that won't make the speaker God's *inerrant spokesperson*. And, if you can find an appropriate scripture, let God speak for himself...he always speaks the truth.

By the way, did you notice the title, *"The Honest Truth?"* There is no truth if it's not honest, and if one is honest, he or she is truthful, right? But, this expression implies that truth has "elbow room," if and when you need some verbal room to move around a bit, you know, to escape getting caught "stretching it" or "softening it." Opinions are generally just that, ideas on things, thoughts about truth, but not cast-in-iron absolutes. Of course, we can always share Scripture with confidence by statements like, "The Bible says," or "I believe the Bible, when it says...."

As I mentioned in another chapter, the scriptures do say that we should speak the truth in "love." This means, of course, that there are times when one should speak the truth in an especially kind or sensitive way to someone. A sickly person, for instance, who you're visiting in the hospital for church asks if the doctor told you that he or she is going to die. You know that the doctor did say he thought it was just a matter of a few days, perhaps a week at best. But, you wouldn't respond to the person's request, for instance, with, "If I were you, Bill, I'd start packing my spiritual suitcase…tonight!" Or, "Yup, he said it looks like tomorrow's a good bet, so what color flowers would you like!" Instead, a truthful but sensitive response might be, "No one knows for sure, Bill, not even your doctor. Things are serious, but let's just keep hoping and praying for the best, okay. God is able to do far more than any of us can ask or think."

The truth is, we ought not to suggest in any way that we know the *specific* time of anyone's death…nor does the doctor, by the way. Love expresses truth with compassion and care.

> *"Everyone enjoys a fitting reply; it is wonderful to say the right thing at the right time!"* (Prov. 15:23 NLT)
>
> *"Let your conversation be always full of grace, seasoned with salt, so that you may know how to answer everyone."* (Col. 4:6 NIV)

Like one wise senator, who spoke criticizingly about the President. He was asked, "So, was the President lying?" The senator's coy response was, "Well, let's say he has trouble with the truth."

One last thing about sharing our thoughts and opinions as God would have us do so. We are accountable for what we say.

> *"A good man brings good things out of the good stored up in him, and an evil man brings evil things out of the evil stored up in him. But I tell you that everyone will have to give account on the day of judgment for every empty word they have spoken. For by your words you will be acquitted, and by your words you will be condemned."* (Matt. 12:35-37)

If we know Christ as Savior and Lord, occasional ill-spoken, harsh, thoughtless and sinful words will not keep us out of heaven any more than occasional sinful behaviors. Christ's blood washes away our guilt regarding our eternal destination. Still, our language and/or opinions reveal the character of who we really are before God. It is also true that believers will face Christ in that Day for how they've lived, which includes words spoken and opinions given. This place of accountability will affect our future rewards and...*I suspect, I believe and I suggest*...that in some way it will also affect our heavenly accommodations and assignments!

Your Spiritual Tool Box

Today's Project:
Words, Ideas and Opinions

Your Blueprint:
"And the words of the LORD are flawless, like silver purified in a crucible, like gold refined seven times." (Psalm 12:6)

Keeping It Plumb:
This program has a spelling and grammar check, but even so, it's amazing how many things it can miss, like to, too, and two. I'm not the best proof reader, so my apologies to those who have found such errors. However, I wish God had giving us a word and opinion checker for reviewing what is about to come out of our mouths! Wouldn't it be great to have a bell sound in our ears, for instance, and a soft voice inside saying, *"Oops...I don't think you want to say that, Ed. A better suggestion would be...."*

Well, that's not in our programming, so we've just got to be cautious, responsible, and clear minded. As the verse says, let's focus upon having a mental "pre-filter" for turning what we're thinking about into words. Thoughtless words, attitudes and opinions can get us into a lot of trouble, and they can also make us people others don't want to be around.

The "Two" of Me

I worked as a representative for an automotive distribution company for about three years. I travelled from dealership to dealership throughout New York State calling on owners and managers to train new employees and to make sure that all advertising materials were properly set up. My direct supervisor for my territory was a believer, and we developed a productive relationship over the years. However, there was supervisor from another district (we'll call him Bob) that just didn't get along with others very well. When I first met him, there seemed to be no problem, for he was cordial and easy to talk with. Still, my supervisor warned me not to "set him off" by doing or saying something that would anger him.

One day, we had to go over to his house to pick up a load of product. I don't remember the specifics, but my supervisor and I probably forgot something we were to bring over, nothing significant. However, Bob became enraged over it. He seemed to change over to another person, and his "nice person" became super judgmental and very angry.

Now, any of us have uncharacteristic reactions and emotions at times, believers or non-believers. But, the *range* of that change reveals a lot of what's going on inside of us. If that swing from controlled and kind swerves dramatically to abusive and nasty often, then we've got significant issues to deal with. In such a case, we might say that two people live within us, and those around us have a very unsettling time waiting to see who will emerge!

In the book of Galatians, Paul says that one of the fruits of the Spirit is self-control. Exercising constraint over our inner person is a *fundamental* part of spiritual obedience, for it affects our witness to others about who Jesus is. In addition, "masking" or "burying" our negative emotions...like anger, fear, guilt...can do great damage to our us and to our bodies (we tend to see spiritual immaturity as something to keep hidden from others, thus hiding our "true" opinions and feelings inside of us). Repressed feelings will eventually "pop up," causing unexpected and unwanted flair-ups of those same buried emotions

We should pray for God's help, when we sense that we're losing control in these areas, and then confess such things as soon as possible. This helps to keep feelings from being masked and causing harm later on. So, ask God for a disciplined mind, but also be willing to share your emotional needs with Him and with other believers for support and encouragement.

"Hey, how are you, Bill?" says Bill's friend, Pete, at church. Bill is feeling guilty about his movie choices last night, about the verbal fight he had with his daughter regarding her promiscuous relationship with her boyfriend, and about the recent loss of his job. But, he doesn't want to bring those things up.

"Great, Pete...life's a bowl of cherries. Why worry about the pits!!!"

Now, everybody is somewhat guarded, just like Pete...and should be...about just dumping a detailed list of *everything* that's going wrong in the lap of someone who's just giving you a friendly greeting. But, if we *seldom acknowledge* our true feelings to ourselves, God or close friends, we are contributing to an unhealthy spiritually. Okay, here's another way we also hide our true self and cause harm.

"So, Mary, what do you think of Angela?" asks Paula as the two of them are talking in the foyer of the youth building.

"Well, she's kind of different, you know what I mean. I'm sure God is going to use her, but...well...minorities always seem to bring some issues into the church." Paula bites her tongue, knowing that the statement is unkind and unfounded. Mary's had this attitude for a while, but, because of their friendship, she's never wanted to confront Mary about it.

"I hear you," she responds.

What's happened here? First, Mary is masking her own feelings about minorities. Perhaps she's toning down her inner prejudice with words like "minorities," when she'd really like to say a particular ethnic background. Or, saying "issues," when at home she'll freely say something much more condemning or judgmental. Then, Paula cops out and masks her own feelings over Mary's self-righteous, perhaps prejudicial attitude. It would be more honest and spiritually obedient to nicely share her displeasure and disappointment regarding her friend's immature perspective.

Things like this happen all the time and can cause genuine problems, which start small in a church's fellowship, but quickly mushroom into rifts of relational separation. For instance, what if Angela's 10 year old daughter happened to go by unnoticed and overheard the conversation as she crossed the foyer? Now the whole thing could spread to another level and more folks would get into gossiping and/or prejudice-driven ways of thinking. Trust me, church splits have come from such things, and the damage to the name of Christ can be significant. Our goal is not to present a "different me," as the need may arise. The goal is to present a single image to others within or without the church, which will glorify God.

So, how many "personalities" live within you? We're not talking about actual personalities, here, just various *masks* we use here and there to cover up our own feelings/opinions. Usually, we use them when asked our opinion about someone or about some issue, and we don't want to answer honestly and forthrightly.

- "So, what do you think about Jennifer...not very mature is she?"
- "You don't like Bill, right? Do you think he's really a Christian?"
- "The Pastor needs to move along. His preaching just stinks!"
- "Politics and religion...they just don't mix, right?"
- "Hey...we all sin. We've just got to love everybody, that's all!"

The human part of Jesus was completely one person, without masks of any sort. He could be as gentle or as tough with people as the need or situation demanded. He wasn't dogmatic and condemning with a repentant prostitute named Mary, nor would he shy away from telling the Pharisees that they were hypocrites and liars. Truth always needs to be said, appropriately, yet compassionately. This is why the Apostle Paul encourages us to, *"speak the truth in love."* Love is never weakened or masked by feelings; it is kind, but also as forthright and firm as it needs to be.

Your Spiritual Tool Box

Today's Project:
Know Who You Are

Your Blueprint:
"...if anyone thinks he is something, when he is nothing, he deceives himself. But let each one test his own work, and then his reason to boast will be in himself alone and not in his neighbor. For each will have to bear his own load." (Gal. 6:3-5 ESV)

Keeping It Plumb:

Years ago, I asked my Youth Director, "Is there a healthy sense of pride?" He wisely said that it's being able to say that the dime in one's hand is never worth only 5 cents or even worth 12 cents. It's just worth 10 cents. Pride enters one's person when you think you're a 12-cent dime! Inferiority sets in when one thinks he or she is nothing more than a 5-cent dime. Know who you are and how God has equipped you to serve him.

Americans spend millions of bucks on health and beauty related products that do nothing but put an unnecessary glow on our outside self in order to impress others. Now, there's nothing wrong with looking your best, and "if the barn needs painting, then paint it," my Pastor would say with a smile. But, beyond that, let's learn to be happy with who we are. Otherwise, we're always trying to be two persons, the one we're chasing around to put in front of others, and the one we really are inside. The first one is fake, the second is the one God created and loves.

Theocracy, Theology and Practicality

*"Do your best to present yourself to God as one approved,
a worker who does not need to be ashamed and who
correctly handles the word of truth."*
(II Timothy 2:15)

When you study the Old Testament, you find that Israel was a theocracy. It meant that the Jewish nation was to be *ruled directly by God*, not by kings or prophets or any other type of political structure. God shared his plan with Abraham:
"...and I will establish my covenant as an everlasting covenant between me and you and your descendants after you for the generations to come, to be your God and the God of your descendants after you." (Gen 17:7)
God spoke directly to him on occasion, as well as to selected kings and prophets at various times in order to give guidance for the Hebrew nation. He would also bring warnings, judgments, deliverances and times of great blessing as he saw fit to do so. As long as the nation maintained its commitment to righteousness and purity, he promised to keep a godly descendent on the throne and practical blessing upon the nation. Unfortunately, Israel often wandered from the teachings of Jehovah and found itself under great chastisement at the hand of God.

Eventually, the Hebrew people decided to live like the nations around it and asked Samuel to provide a king to rule its land. Though this offended both Samuel and the Lord, God allowed it to take place. Later on, the people eventually learned how difficult and painful it was to place self-centered and self-serving kings in the place of God, because of their tendency toward idolatry and spiritual wickedness.

The church is not a political theocracy, but it is a *spiritual* theocracy. In other words, we as believers both individually and corporately seek the counsel and direction of Almighty God. He alone is our "executive/supervisor/manager," and we want to follow his leadership in all things. Yes, God has chosen that there should be Pastors, Elders, and various types of leaders as "under-shepherds" to supervise the work of the church. But, all of the people and its leaders follow the Scriptures for their authority in worship and in life.

This requires, of course, that we understand who God is and what is required of individual believers and the body of Christ, the church, on this earth. The first way we do involves *theology*, where we search the scriptures in order to define sound and systematic Biblical doctrines. Doctrines are threads of Biblical truth and teaching critical to our overall understanding of life. Here's a few fundamental teachings and/or doctrines to review.

FUNDAMENTAL DOCTRINES

APOSTLE: Apostle means one who is sent; a messenger. The 12 disciples were also called Apostles. The Apostle Paul, for instance, was called by the Lord to establish small churches after Jesus' death and also wrote much of the New Testament. The Bible says that the church is "built" upon the Apostles' teaching (the twelve). The last Apostle was John, who wrote a Gospel, 3 New Testament letters and the book of Revelation.

ATONEMENT: Christ's substitutionary death on the cross has *satisfied* God's displeasure and anger over our sinful lifestyle. His blood on the cross makes eternal "atonement" for our guilt, because we trusted in Christ as personal Savior and Lord. As believers, we no longer are held in the merciless grip of death.

FAITH: The decision to believe that Jesus is the Son of God and to trust in His sacrificial death upon the cross for personal forgiveness and salvation. This act of faith is accompanied by living in obedience to the will of God found in the Bible.

CHURCH: The church is the "gathering" of believers for weekly fellowship, teaching and encouragement. It is not a building or a room, but the people of God, who believe in Jesus as Savior and Lord. The Holy Spirit individually dwells within each one of us.

BORN AGAIN: Being "born again" is what Jesus referred to as what happens when a person believes in Christ Jesus as Lord and Savior. It refers to being born spiritually to a *new life with God*. It's another term for being *"saved."*

FELLOWSHIP: Fellowship is the common spiritual bond and relationship all believers have with each other. It also refers to the way we help and learn from one another, as we meet regularly for support and encouragement.

GOSPEL: The Gospel means "good news" and incorporates the following truths:
1. Our sin separated us from God the Father (*depravity*) and targets us for eternal punishment (*hell*).
2. But, God loved us so much that he sent Jesus, His sinless Son, to die a *substitutionary* death on a Roman cross...*in place of us*. That death satisfied God's anger for all our guilt and sin (*propitiation, atonement*).
3. Those who accept this and ask God to personally forgive them because of Jesus' death (*saving faith*), are put in right standing with God (*justification*). Their relationship with God is restored (*reconciliation*), and will eventually spend eternity with Jesus, who awaits them in heaven.

SCRIPTURE: The Bible is completely trustworthy and written by godly, chosen people as they were "moved" and inspired by the Holy Spirit. It contains 27 New Testament books and 39 Old Testament books and is the only genuine foundation for the church. It is fully trustworthy and exists as the single, ruling standard for our spiritual lives (the *canon*). The Word of God was given and written down (*revelation*) by prophets and apostles under the authoritative and errorless oversight of the Holy Spirit (*inspiration*).

[The Roman Catholic church added 7 non-canonical books (known as the Apocrypha) at the council of Trent in 1546 AD. However, these "apocryphal books" were never accepted by Jesus or the early church as trustworthy. They were added by the Roman church, frankly, to support its spurious doctrines added over the years (e.g. Mariology, purgatory, mortal/venial sins, papal succession, indulgences, among others). They have many errors, spurious fantasy type stories, and they contain doctrines incongruent the rest of the Bible and sound doctrine]

GRACE: God's loving-kindness toward anyone, which is rich in forgiveness and acceptance ((*expiation*). Believers have entered into an *ongoing relationship* with God (*regeneration*), because *of God's mercy*. His loving-kindness has forgiven all their sin and guilt...a precious gift. It is not earned or deserved, just received by faith in Jesus Christ. Though we receive this salvation by "unmerited grace," our good works do prove the *authenticity* of one's faith.

HEAVEN: A place reserved for those who have chosen to believe in God, his Truth and his Son, the Lord Jesus. It is a life of eternal bliss with Christ and with those who have similarly followed God's will.

HELL: A place reserved for evil and evil doers, including Satan and all of his demons (the fallen angels, who serve him). It is a place of conscious suffering and spiritual loneliness for those who reject God, his Truth and his Son.

HOLY: Holy means "separate." God is holy, pure, and *separate from sin* in His basic character. *He cannot do wrong.* Similarly, believers are called to live holy (or godly) lives as followers of Jesus Christ (sanctification).

INSPIRATION: God spoke to the hearts and minds of chosen individuals in Old Testament and New Testament days. He caused them to write down his words accurately in their own language and style for all of us to read. The Bible is God's trustworthy and "inspired" Word in order for us to find comfort, help and instruction in how to live the Christian life.

PROPHET: One specially called by God to speak for Him *directly*. A prophet doesn't teach what he understands about God alone, but spoke *specifically* what God wanted him to say. Old Testament prophets (e.g. Isaiah) also proclaim God's plan for the future.

RECONCILED: Because of what Jesus did on the cross, believers have been "reconciled" or *restored* to an intimate relationship with God. The Holy Spirit has been given to them and they can confidently talk with God in prayer and listen to Him talk to them through the pages of God's Word, the Bible.

SAVED: Jesus' death has "saved" us from the God's anger regarding our sinful attitudes and choices. Through faith and repentance, God forgives us and comes to indwell us. We have been set free from the penalty of sin and will live forever in heaven with Jesus, instead of Hell.

SAINTS: The Bible refers to all believers as "saints," a term used by the Apostle Paul in the early church. Though some refer to saints as special people with some degree of miraculous-type work in their lives, such is not the *specific* meaning of the Biblical term. *Anyone* who has trusted in Christ for salvation can rightly be called a saint.

SIN: Disobedience to God's moral demands and "missing the mark" of his will in attitude and behavior. Sin is also a "condition" in which non-Christians find themselves in relation to God. Apart from a relationship with Jesus, all people are separated from God and morally accountable for their wrong attitudes and choices. Creation itself is marred by this "state of sin," meaning it exists in an imperfect and physically corrupted environment.

SATAN: Also called the Devil. A powerful spiritual being, who rebelled against God ages ago. He roams the world, fostering spiritual disruption, evil behavior and ultimate loss of eternal life. Though allowed to live for a time, God has condemned him to eternal death.

WORSHIP: Worship is giving God praise for who He is and what He is doing for us. It also involves thanking Him for his loving kindness in providing for our needs and protecting us from evil. Examples are people worshipping the Lord in prayer and song

PRACTICAL THEOLOGY

Secondly, theology is never meant to be *impractical*. Yes, it can be a bit more "heady" ("theology" is defined as the study of God). Nevertheless, understanding it and *applying* it has important ramifications for every believer. In this more general sense, then, there are "non-theological" concepts, principles and teachings that must be understood and *applied* to our daily lives, if we are to live a godly and successful Christian life.

Look at it this way. The *doctrine* of atonement has important implications for daily living, but we must realize that this doesn't mean we never sin any more. It simply means that the wrath of God, capable of sending us to hell, has been *satisfied* and *appeased* by Christ's death.

> "...*by one sacrifice he has made perfect forever those who are being made holy."* (Hebrews 10:14)

Our destination will no longer be hell, for our sins are no longer holding us accountable to God...we are forgiven.

However, practically speaking, Christ's atonement makes God's powerful resources available by prayer, as we approach God's throne of grace with confidence in order to find God's "...*mercy and find grace to help us in our time of need."* (Hebrews 4:16) So, atonement is not an excuse to sin, but it is good to know that my daily failures can be dealt with confidently, because of Christ's sacrifice upon the cross. There is no need to carry around unnecessary guilt, shame, depression or self-rejection because of nagging sinful acts or attitudes. Though our daily lives may be soiled with occasional sin, our *relationship* with God is non-alterable for all eternity.

So, you can see how the doctrine of atonement lays a healthy foundation, after which practical teaching must step in to assist for our ongoing spiritual growth. And, there is a whole area of supportive teaching that the Scriptures provide, which are less "theological" and more "practical" for believers. All of it is God's Truth, so get into it and let the Spirit of God transform you with it over time, as you apply both doctrine and practical teaching to your life.

Your Spiritual Tool Box

Today's Project:
Sound Doctrine

Your Blueprint:
*"Since an overseer manages God's household, he must be blameless—not overbearing, not quick-tempered, not given to drunkenness, not violent, not pursuing dishonest gain.
Rather, he must be hospitable, one who loves what is good, who is self-controlled, upright, holy and disciplined.
He must hold firmly to the trustworthy message as it has been taught,* **so that he can encourage others by sound doctrine and refute those who oppose it."** (Titus 1:7-9)

Keeping It Plumb:
Ever hear of those Mississippi boatmen who took "soundings" of the river as they maneuvered through frequently shallow waters? They wanted to make sure the waters were deep enough for the boat to travel down river without scrapping the bottom. Sound doctrine implies teaching that is deeply Biblical, doctrinally trustworthy, and spiritually reliable for believers to travel down the road of life within the will of God.

Biting The Bait

Temptation is something all believers must face and learn how to combat successfully. God has also given us his Holy Spirit in order to provide the strength and stamina to overcome it. But, some temptations seem too difficult to ignore or reject, and we just "bite the bait" once again. This, of course, is what temptation is all about - feeling or wanting something that you shouldn't feel or want in kind or degree, thereby *being drawn* toward the unwanted behavior. If we keep indulging ourselves in sin, over time we'll completely handicap the capacity of our will to choose to obey God.

    I remember canoeing alongside a lake in Canada at our yearly men's retreat at church. I through the line in along the underwater rocks and waited. It took only a matter of seconds and my lure was hit by a good-sized bass. I pulled it in, but had to put it back into the water, because it was out of season. Then, I threw in another line with my favorite lure. Wammo! Another hit, but this time the fish actually jumped out of the water, and I noticed that I had hooked the *same fish!*

Rip....the line suddenly went limp, and that fish swam away with my favorite lure still in its mouth. I told myself this is not going to happen, so I quickly reloaded my line with another lure and threw it back into the water, hoping to catch the same fish with my lure still stuck in its mouth. A minute went by and...wammo! Again, that crazed fish attacked my line. I cautiously tried to pull it in, but this time the fish jumped out of the water, twisted violently, and *threw my favorite lure back into the canoe!* I couldn't believe it! What was with that crazy fish?

Spiritually speaking, there is always a "mental trigger" or thought pattern that can "lure" us into sinful indulgence, whether physical or attitudinal. With *some* temptations, simply refusing to think about a particular passion will "un-cock the trigger," thereby *defusing* the unwanted desire or emotion, and thus avoiding sin (this assumes, of course, that there is already a *resident reservoir* of commitment able to resist that inclination).

Many times, however, that reservoir of godly intention is just *too low* to resist temptation. It's rather like pressing your thumb on a leaky faucet. No matter how slow the leak, you just can't stop the flow...the pressure builds and builds, eventually jetting out from beneath your thumb. And, once again, we sin.

Sometimes, our spiritual, physical or emotional "lure" has been so well embedded into our psyche that throwing the mental lure back into the boat is just too difficult. Perhaps our passions are *too enflamed* from previously inappropriate thought patterns, either by childhood or adulthood indiscretions. Like a bad tooth infection, habit has enrooted itself, and we lack enough spiritual resolve or godly conviction to win over it. So, we just *bite into that sin* – gambling, porn, alcohol, stealing, credit card abuse, gluttony, etc. - again and again. Our spiritual sensitivities have been *dulled* to the point that we are unable to exert significant control over our evil impulses. A particular sin has now become uncomfortably *repetitive*, and our "hair trigger" fires off a sinful attitude or action without much struggle at all.

The point is that when a passion has been repetitively indulged in, one's thoughts can unleash a powerful, pent-up flow of sinful impulses, which the will finds hard to ignore. Again, this could be anger turned into violence; pride turned into prejudice; lust turned into bondage; hunger turned into gluttony; self-hate turned into bulimia – you name it. Regardless, simple thought manipulation alone seldom wins many races in such situations, though it may help, of course. Only deep **attitudinal** change at the level of our impassioned beliefs will break Satan's grip.

So, let's get practical...if you don't want to bite into the bait, then you've got to change what's going on inside of you. The lure of the bait can only be overcome by increasing one's desire for God, such that the lure loses its power over us. We've got to develop an **impassioned determination** to seek and serve God that is so overwhelming it overpowers the alluring lust of evil. And, like that fish, we're able to spit it out of our lives, because of the pain and discomfort it brings.

Now, the above usually requires a process and a learning curve, though God can immediately eliminate certain undesirable lures from our life, if he chooses to do so. However, that is not the norm. Most often, he is more interested in transforming our own inner person, than he is in simply surgically removing the evil desire or intent. *Fundamentally speaking,* as we discussed before, such a transformation requires three things:

- Repentant faith in Jesus Christ
- Wanting God and seeking his will
- Surrendering to God and his will

This remains a critical order for spiritual change to occur. Spiritual change and growth always begins with heart conviction, activated and impassioned by God's Spirit and Word, until our heart surrenders itself to the will of God.

At the core of it all is our faith...our love for Jesus as Savior and Lord. This is the footing upon which we build our spiritual house, but it's also the reliable platform of desire and determination to which we must return, when overcoming the lure of sin. As we return again and again to a place of *complete consecration* in order to renew our hearts in the strength of His Spirit, only then will we more consistently "throw the lure" back into the boat of evil.

I've watched professional fighters win a fight handily over an opponent. But, after a brief lay off from all the physical preparation and discipline, they'll get right into it again in order to get ready for the next challenger. Similarly, spiritual victories are achieved by *sustained* intensity and effort. By this, I don't mean simple determination and human effort, I mean ongoing, faith initiated, passion driven intimacy with Jesus Christ. The world's activities can easily dull and diminish our spiritual prowess, and only our abiding Savior within can keep our intensity deep and strong for the next battle. So, stay close, friend, to the Savior who loves you in order to draw enough inner grace and power to resist Satan's devices. Seek God continually in this way and remember II Chronicles 15:15:

"...they sought God eagerly and he was found by them."

Your Spiritual Tool Box

Today's Project:
Cut The Line!

Your Blueprint:
"...if your right hand causes you to stumble, cut it off and throw it away. It is better for you to lose one part of your body than for your whole body to go into hell." (Matt. 5:30)

Keeping It Plumb:

Let's change the example of the fish being lured by the bait and repetitively biting into it. What about the situation when a *fisherman* hooks *himself* into something he doesn't want to be hooked into...like a tree, some sea weed, or perhaps a snapping turtle, for instance? The only thing one can do is cut the line, for the line has entangled itself mercilessly. Well, sometimes we "hook" a sin in our daily lives, perhaps by watching television in a hotel room alone, or listening to a persuasive non-believer, or allowing our anger to vent itself unwisely...whatever. Ignore it all you want or hope it will free itself eventually. But, the truth is, *it just won't let go on its own!* Especially with potentially habitual sins, we've got to ask God for the power to disengage ourselves spiritually from every mental hook which ties us to sinful entanglements or harmful predators. In other words, we've got too cut the line! This means breaking all contacts, relationships, fantasies, or memories that continue to grip us, then focusing upon God's Word and the Spirit's inner promptings toward godliness and purity. Cut the line, friend, before *you're* the one that gets bitten!

How Deep Is Your Well?

When I was growing up in rural Connecticut, we had an artesian well in the back near the woods. As I said before, we lived in a cabin for several months while my parents built the new house around it. You had to energetically pump that big, iron arm in order to draw the cool underground water to the surface from 175' below. Well water was always the best, because it had innate properties, loaded with minerals, and it was good for one's health. I'd like to apply that old well to the Christian life and garner some *fundamental* principles of spiritual growth.

First, it took some significant effort to get the pump to bring the water to the surface. Similarly, getting to know Christ more deeply involves some *focused effort,* for God asks this from anyone that wants to know him better. A non-believer has to begin *searching* for God, if he or she wants to find him. The Bible says:

"You will seek me and find me when you seek me with all your heart."
(Jeremiah 29:13)

The problem with many people who say they'd like to know God is that they're not willing to genuinely reach out and seek him. God will not turn away a truly searching soul from finding him, for he honors such a spark of faith. If a person is willing to start "pumping" after God, he will reward his efforts. I believe that God's Spirit is forever moving over the face of mankind, gently calling at times and loudly shouting at other times, trying to draw people to himself...if only they would truly reach out for him in sincerity and faith.

The first three chapters in the book of Romans clearly talks about this, declaring that God is not holding anyone back from believing and receiving him into their lives. I know of many Muslims, for instance, who lived in a completely "darkened" world, spiritually speaking, who reached out for God to show himself to them. And, through God's amazing and sovereign leading through the means of visions and circumstances, Christ brought the Gospel to them in order to find salvation.

For believers, too, the well of God in Christ Jesus is equally full of mercy, grace and empowerment. But, it is equally important that we energetically reach out to God with desire and determination, if we are to have him fill our lives. Lazy believers get little from the well of salvation....saved, yes, but lacking so much more that God has for them, if they would only reach out energetically to get it.

Let me change the example of the well just a bit. Let's say that the well is our own heart, and its depth indicates how much we love Jesus and want him to please him in our lives. Thus, a deeply dug well indicates a great love for the things of Christ, while a shallow dug well indicates less love for the things of God. Here are three, fundamental principles I can draw from this analogy. First...

Personal Depth

How deep is my love for Jesus, my Savior and Lord? Jesus taught a parable about a farmer who sowed seed, but the crops that the seed produced varied in growth. Some seed produced 30 times what was sown, some 60 times sown and others 100 times what was sown. He was saying that not everyone will be as "fruitful" in their commitment to Christ as others. The reason is that the more productive seed was more deeply sown into the heart of his hearers.

> *"But the seed falling on good soil refers to someone who hears the word and understands it. This is the one who produces a crop, yielding a hundred, sixty or thirty times what was sown."* (Matthew 13:23)

In addition, part of our relationship with God evidences itself in a spiritual thirst for greater knowledge and wisdom. I don't mean to say that every believer has to have the depth of a Pastor in these areas, but he or she does need to understand spiritual realities and the principles of God's Word. This is a sign of spiritual maturity, for those that are stuck in sin or living lackadaisical lives for Christ are probably there in large part because of a *shallow commitment* to Biblical study. Our love for Christ must drive us deep into the Scriptures, where God's life changing wisdom and knowledge dwell.

To summarize, a well that is full of spiritual sustenance is one that has been dug deeply into the heart. And, because of this, the person's life is full of spiritual fruit. In such a life, I would see that person having a strong devotional life, taking the time to search the Scriptures for God's truth and applying it to his or her life. I would also find this person able to worship God with genuine praise and thanksgiving, as well as enjoying the fellowship of the church on a consistent basis. He or she would similarly be living close to God and in this way regularly confessing personal sins and maintaining an intimate relationship with Christ.

Relational Depth

Mature believers seek opportunities to share their faith with others around them where ever they might be, as well as serving the Lord in some personal ministry in the church. But, most importantly, they would model the love of Christ in those relationships with a sincere and ever-deepening desire to care for others.

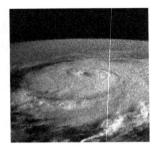

I have the pleasure of knowing a wonderful couple, Matt and Annette, who live in Florida. Matt is a carpenter and assisted in the rebuilding process after the devastating effects of Hurricane Katrina in 2005. He has demonstrated his sincere compassion for others by going into the devastated areas caused by that storm in order to bring encouragement and rebuilding assistance. Since then, the fall onslaught of the 2017 season will find them this couple very much involved, I'm sure, in the rebuilding effort.

But, there are many relationships that test and/or reveal the quality of our love for Jesus. For instance,

- Is my love for Christ evident in the way I relate and make decisions in my family life...with my spouse and children?
- Is my love for Christ seen by those with whom I work, or am I more of a good "talker" and less of a "walker," when it comes to my faith?
- Is my love for Christ acknowledged by my church family. Do they see that I spend significant time in ministering to others in my gift areas?

Overall, then, each of us are at various depths in our walk with God. This is why Jeremiah says, *"The heart is deceitful above all things and beyond cure. Who can understand it? I the LORD search the heart and examine the mind, to reward each person according to their conduct, according to what their deeds deserve."* (Jer. 17:9,10)

Your Spiritual Tool Box

Today's Project:
Reaching Up

Your Blueprint:
"So then, just as you received Christ Jesus as Lord, continue to live your lives in him, rooted and built up in him, strengthened in the faith as you were taught, and overflowing with thankfulness." (Col. 2:6, 7)

Keeping It Plumb:

I like the word, "rooted." Though it could remind me of a tooth being yanked from its deep grip upon one's jaw by a skilled Dentist, it most often reminds me of a plant or tree. One such tree I saw in the woods near a friend's house as we were walking along a field. This large, 4" thick branch emerged from the edge of the woods and went straight up toward the sky. As stopped to look at it, I noticed that it was attached to another branch about 10 inches thick, which ran parallel to the ground from inside the woods, so I followed it. That branch went about 10 feet along the ground to a modest sized tree amid many others nearby. However, it really seemed dwarfed by the others, because the woods were so thick. Apparently, this tree couldn't get enough light, so it reached out through the other trees into the field, then sprang upward toward the sun in order to gain the light it needed to grow. What a great

picture of our need to reach out to God in every way in order to gain the sustenance and strength for our own spiritual growth.

Learning To Love

"On one occasion an expert in the law stood up to test Jesus. "Teacher," he asked, "what must I do to inherit eternal life?" "What is written in the Law?" he replied. "How do you read it?" He answered, "'Love the LORD your God with all your heart and with all your soul and with all your strength and with all your mind'; and, 'Love your neighbor as yourself.'" "You have answered correctly," Jesus replied. "Do this and you will live." But he wanted to justify himself, so he asked Jesus, "And who is my neighbor?" In reply Jesus said: "A man was going down from Jerusalem to Jericho, when he was attacked by robbers. They stripped him of his clothes, beat him and went away, leaving him half dead. A priest happened to be going down the same road, and when he saw the man, he passed by on the other side. So too, a Levite, when he came to the place and saw him, passed by on the other side. But a Samaritan, as he traveled, came where the man was; and when he saw him, he took pity on him. He went to him and bandaged his wounds, pouring on oil and wine. Then he put the man on his own donkey, brought him to an inn and took care of him. The next day he took out two denarii and gave them to the innkeeper. 'Look after him,' he said, 'and when I return, I will reimburse you for any extra expense you may have.' "Which of these three do you think was a neighbor to the man who fell into the hands of robbers?" The expert in the law replied, "The one who had mercy on him." Jesus told him, "Go and do likewise." (Luke 10:25-37)

One of the most *fundamental* elements of the Christian life is love. However, when I thought about it and tried to come up with examples of it, I was stymied.

Yes, general acts of kindness crossed my mind, which is loving behavior, of course, but I really couldn't find very graphic and profound examples. Then I remembered the story above about the great love shown by the travelling Samaritan man, who stopped and helped a wounded Levite, with whom he would not normally socialize. His compassion and commitment to that unfortunate man is one of the finest examples of genuine love. Here's why I think so.

LOVE COSTS...

King David wanted to offer a sacrifice on a piece of land owned by Araunah, a *Jebusite*. He was willing to pay for it, but Araunah refused it at first. David was so sorrowful, however, because of the sinful and prideful counting of his armed forces, that he demanded he be allowed to pay for it.

"...the king replied to Araunah, "No, I insist on paying you for it. I will not sacrifice to the Lord my God burnt offerings that cost me nothing."

So David bought the threshing floor and the oxen and paid fifty shekels of silver for them. David built an altar to the Lord there and sacrificed burnt offerings and fellowship offerings. Then the Lord answered his prayer in behalf of the land, and the plague on Israel was stopped." (II Samuel 24:24)

The key principle is that the deepest form of love is sacrificial, it costs something. A person truly loves someone else when he or she is willing to give up something normally very precious or desirable in order to show that love. David loved God deeply and showed it by paying a significant price as part of his repentance for doing something detestable in the eyes of God. He had begun to trust in his own power and ingenuity, without fully acknowledging God's sovereign blessing in his life. Many people lost their lives because of David's pride that day. His repentance, though not entirely free from God's judgment, proved itself sincere and acceptable before God and avoided further loss.

Simple kindness is wonderful and loving, but sometimes the cost of love becomes more expensive for the giver. It's then that we must ask the question of ourselves: "Are we willing to practice the type of love for God and others that may cost us even everything we own?"

> *"For the love of Christ controls us, because we have concluded this: that one has died for all, therefore all have died; and he died for all, that those who live might no longer live for themselves but for him who for their sake died and was raised."* (II Corinthians 5:14, 15)

LOVE ACTS

Love may involve our feelings, of course, where we are emotionally touched by someone's loss, financial struggle, sickness or other serious type of situation. But, in the end, it is what we actually do that reveals the essence and integrity of genuine love.

A number of years ago, a good friend, Abe, was asked by his ailing brother if he would be willing to give up one of his kidneys so that he might live. There was no other medicine or operation at the time other than a kidney transplant that could save Abe's brother's life. Abe did so, even though the operation was a painful one with significant recuperation required later on.

The thing that was remarkable was Abe's almost immediate attitude of compassion and willingness. I'm sure he must have sincerely considered his choice to do so in light of his family and work-related needs first, but his love for his brother still remained a priority. I don't believe that *feelings* ultimately caused him to say yes. Rather, it was a sincere, intentional act of profound **responsibility** to give up something of *great value* in order to significantly help someone in *great need*. Though many often talk about this type of giving, Abe genuinely practiced it and acted upon his convictions. In my mind, he remains a person possessing genuine love.

LOVE ACCEPTS

I wonder if Jesus sat down at one time with the Father…say around King David's time…and the Father asked him, "This world looks kind of bad, don't you think? Israel is so backslidden, you may have to go down there in person. What's your thinking?"

"Well…it wouldn't be a good scenario, that's for sure," Jesus responds. "I mean, I'd enjoy the teaching and the discipleship training, of course. But…I don't know. I'm certainly willing to die for these folks, if absolutely necessary, but they really are quite an ugly, unappreciative and stubborn-hearted bunch of carnally focused sinners. Oh…I suppose…I guess I could do so, but only if you want me to do so."

Actually, I don't wonder about it at all, for Jesus never vacillated in his love for us. He knew before he created us, that he would need to die for us on a Roman cross in order to save us from our sins…*and he still created us!* Think about that.

"Blessed be the God and Father of our Lord Jesus Christ, who has blessed us in Christ with every spiritual blessing in the heavenly places,

> *even as he chose us in him before the foundation of the world, that we should be holy and blameless before him. In love..."* (Eph. 1:4)

Love doesn't concern itself very much with the condition or character of the person who needs its help. It accepts the person for who his is...sinner or saint...and readily responds.

> *"Love is patient, love is kind. It does not envy, it does not boast, it is not proud. It does not dishonor others, it is not self-seeking, it is not easily angered, it keeps no record of wrongs. Love does not delight in evil but rejoices with the truth. It always protects, always trusts, always hopes, always perseveres."* (1 Corinthians 13:4-6)

When a fellow soldier in a foxhole sees a grenade drop alongside his buddy, his love won't ask, "Is he good enough to die for?" He simple responds and gives up his life in an instant in order that his fellow soldier might live.

I was traveling for a company in the country one day, when I turned down a sparsely populated country road. It was a beautiful summer day and cloudless. Suddenly, as I came over a small hill, I saw a single farm house with a barn next to it, which was in flames...I mean roaring, high reaching tongues of fire! I stopped the car by the mail box, about 30 feet from the house, which itself was only 30 feet from the engulfed barn. I felt the intense heat and heard all kinds of crackling and

popping sounds. Just outside the barn and next to the house was a car, and I was aware that the gas tank could probably explode at any moment from the intense heat and flames that were now licking against the side of the house. Though I was concerned about the imminent danger, I could only think that perhaps a small child or injured parent was in there, helpless and unable to escape. So, I asked the Lord to protect me and ran into the house through the open front door, scanning the downstairs area and shouting, "Is anyone here?" There was no answer to my repeated shouts, so I ran back outside, but turned around to the side of the house, still shouting. As I looked into the large field next to the house, I noticed two young pre-teens huddling together about half a football field away. I yelled to them, and they shouted back that they were okay. It was about that time that the police and fire trucks arrived, so I spent a while sharing what I was doing there and then left a half hour later. I'm not suggesting that this was in any sense an act of love, frankly, but it reminds me that sometimes we *spontaneously act* in our efforts to help out someone in need.

Consider this...when a child is inside of a burning house and you are locked out of the front door, will you worry about whether or not there's a locked door or how much pain you might have to face to get inside? No...you will get in there, no matter what! Nothing could keep you out. In the same way, *genuine love* accepts the person, in spite of whether or not you like him. You simply act upon what is right and good and responsible. Jesus knew the sinners we would become before he formed us in our mother's womb...and he still died for us and brought us to faith. That's unselfish and compassionate love that should be a fundamental goal each and every day for us. Let's, "Go and do thou likewise."

Your Spiritual Tool Box

Today's Project:
Responsive or Responsible Love

Your Blueprint:
*"If you love those who love you, what credit is that to you?
Even sinners love those who love them."*
(Luke 6:32)

Keeping It Plumb:
I remember a marital counselor who thought it critical for all spouses to distinguish between these two concepts above, if they desired a long lasting, happy marriage. *Responsive love* can be kind and giving to a point, but it wants to stop when the other person is unkind, forgetful or antagonistic. However, *Responsible love* doesn't care about those things, for it simply acts, seeking to please God and help others "without strings." It seems an impossible task for our humanity to take on, but in Christ all things are possible. So, let's pray and seek the Holy Spirit's resources to genuinely and profoundly be *Christ-like in all of our relationships.*

"I can do all things through Christ which strengthens me." (Phil. 4:13)

Servanthood and Ministry

A *fundamental* responsibility of the Christian life is to be a willing servant through whom God can work and minister effectively. Believers tend to get the order wrong, assuming that the Pastor does the work of ministry, while they enjoy listening to his sermons and attending fellowship gatherings for spiritual encouragement. In reality, however, God has called each one of us into ministry, helping others in areas of need and involved with the church in the areas of our giftedness. We must see ourselves as servants of Jesus Christ, who are willing to serve him by serving others. One believer might teach, another encourages, someone else might provide financial support, while still another just faithfully helps out at the church. All are to be servants at heart, willing to minister to the needs of others in any reasonable and responsible way they can. Let's explore some obvious ways this can be done.

ENCOURAGING

So many of us...all of us at times...can be beaten down by the cares of life. Financial pressures, loss of special people, job responsibilities, educational challenges, family issues...all of these can at times weigh very heavily upon our minds and hearts. One who sees his role as someone who has a good word for

others all the time can be greatly used in the church; he or she is can uplift them and help them to bear their difficult life burdens. Proverbs 25:11 says:
"A word fitly spoken is like apples of gold in a setting of silver."

TEACHING

There's great joy in presenting God's Truth, especially when you see someone's eyes light up with a deeper understanding of Scripture. You've given them a tasty bit of spiritual insight to nibble upon, hoping that it will also bring helpful change in his or her walk with Christ.

Teaching, of course, is a main focus in all churches, for it is meant to inspire, instruct and impact our lives for Jesus. Small group leaders are involved preparing and delivering their weekly lessons at church or in homes in order to strengthen the faith and the fellowship fabric of the congregation. Sunday School teachers, VBS teachers, youth group leaders, college age/young adult groups, senior citizen groups, couples' groups, singles' groups, outreach groups, discipleship groups, etc., all attempt to meet the pressing needs of a growing church.

At our church, we have a "Free Indeed" group on Monday nights, for instance, which is open for those struggling with addictions of any kind. Similar to AA meetings, it offers weekly accountability and support to those who reach out for such help. We also have a Camping Group of 150+ members that enjoy a week every summer in the Adirondacks. It's not just for fun, for they take turns having daily devotions and fellowship times, too. Both are wonderful opportunities to both serve and be served.

One helpful tidbit about teaching: *it's not just telling.* Anyone can tell someone something they themselves have read in a book or in the Bible...more is required. For the truth to really take hold in someone's life, it needs relational encouragement and creative, practical application. One can dump a truck load of loom on a dried up, unproductive landscape and throw some seed on it. But, it's not going to grow much grass unless you spread the seed around and work the seed into the loom with a rake. Similarly, God's truth needs some spiritual raking to make the seed go deep into a person's heart soil. That's accomplished by showing genuine love and transparency, using plenty of real life examples, and following up appropriately, as the need appears.

VISITING

Here's another one of those things we think is only for Pastors...visiting homes or people in hospitals. Again, the reality is that we as "lay leaders" can easily visit someone by just making a phone call. For instance, I called a friend yesterday, who hasn't been around for a few Sundays and missed a couple of Men's Bible studies in a row. I was concerned and gave him a call just to check on things and make sure I wasn't missing something like a loss in the family or some sort of prolonged sickness. He said that he had just been unusually busy getting his summer cottage ready for the winter. It even meant he had to go to an earlier service on Sundays in order to travel down to the camp site and have most of the day to work on it. I was relieved and glad to hear that things were fine with him and his family. And, he was happy that I had taken the time to care.

Of course, older folks, who are stuck in their home for some physical issue, usually enjoy a friendly visit as well. Also, there are people recuperating at home or being attended to at the hospital, who also are greatly uplifted by a phone call, an email, a letter, a text, or a personal visit. Let's not be so busy that we fail to be in touch with those around us in the body of Christ and miss opportunities to share the love of Christ *when life begins to hurt.* To some degree, the Lord will hold us accountable for being too busy to care for others in need *whose lives touch ours.*

HELPING

A gift of "helps" is so important, for it facilitates fellowship-related tasks and oversees the physical maintenance of the church building. For instance, people who are good at administration and organization are able to handle record keeping and office maintenance, communicational pieces, small group oversight, parishioner feedback, prayer requests, hospital visit assignments/results, and various leadership assigned tasks/initiatives. Creative folks can provide pastoral support for presentational power points, HO's, and a wide variety of resource materials for teaching and general information. People skilled in facility maintenance can help the church save money in areas of plumbing, carpentry and electrical repair. Even more so, they can also help folks out that are struggling financially, providing affordable assistance in areas of home maintenance. Some of the guys at our church, for instance, have a monthly day at the church, where they can do the small things for no charge, like replacing mufflers and brake pads, changing spark plugs and fluids, rotating tires, etc.

Lastly, we have a new ministry we've started recently...a 5K race held each October, which is open to the community. My friend, Rob, saw the need for our church to reach out to the community and let them know in a strategic way that we're here. We have the support of area businesses and offer prizes for both age and time, along with plenty of after race food and fun. We're well over 100 runners coming each year from within a 15-mile radius! Another opportunity for people to help and assist in the delivery of this fine outreach event.

Look around at your church, and you'll generally find a group of reliable helpers, always ready to put away chairs after meetings, help cook meals for special events, and perform clean up duties. We have a Halloween night alternative at our church, called Fall Fest, which requires a lot of helpers to faithfully sweep up the hay, clean up the lawns after the horses, goats and sheep have gone. Others re-package the air-filled jumping attractions, provide drinks and snacks, run games, take care of health-related needs/accidents, and welcome and record visitors We also have a security team that has strategic places of oversight at all church events...just in case (I'm exhausted just thinking about it all!). You can see that a church without gifted helpers "applying their trade" isn't going to be very large or effective in today's world.

I could go on, but I think the point is clear. There's plenty of *responsibility* and *opportunity* in your church and mine to become involved....and, frankly, it's really not a choice...God asks all of us to spend time doing "ministry" in the areas of our gifts. And, when we've gotten into a special area of ministry, I really believe that it can minister to us even more than it does to those we happen to be serving. When so involved, we're focused, prayerful and very cognizant of our need to be spiritually close to Christ...and that's what it's all about!

Your Spiritual Tool Box

Today's Project:
Gifted and Involved

Your Blueprint:
"Now to each one the manifestation of the Spirit Is given for the common good." (I Cor. 12:7)

Keeping It Plumb:
No one can say he or she is left out of this blessing or responsibility. All of us have been spiritually equipped and given enough life experience to serve God and others, ministering to folks through the power of God's indwelling Spirit.

Final Thoughts: Giving It Your All

"The World Has Not Yet Seen One Totally Committed to God"

The weather was great....80 degrees on a cloudless day at the beach. Our church youth group had planned this Saturday outing for a couple of months, and we were out to have a blast. Eighty teenagers arrived in cars stuffed with food, volleyballs, flippers, face masks...and lots of food!

It was about an hour to get to the beach from the church, but the joking around and the excitement made the trip seem just around the corner. We were one of the first cars to arrive and pulled up to the guard house, paid our parking fee, and slowly made our way to the beach parking lot. There was a slight breeze, which moved the tall grass back and forth along the narrow, sand swept macadam road. I was driving and spotted a lone parking space up ahead, so I gunned it to get there before anyone else. I parked and quickly held down the button on the locks to keep everyone inside for the fun of it.

"Hey, Kenerson...what are ya doing? Let us out of here, will ya!" So, I stopped, opened up my door and jumped out ahead of everyone. My riders jumped out after me and ran to the trunk to get all their stuff. Some of the kids were already in their bathing suits, but some had to go and put them on at the changing area at the main concession building.

Within an hour, all eighty of us had found a comfortable spot on the beach, created a place for cooking the hot dogs and hamburgers, and then jumped into the frothy waves. Because this was the Connecticut shoreline in late August, the water temperature was only in the low seventies, but it was still great to be jumping around in it. Of course, some of the teens were playing with frisbees and others were just walking along the water's edge looking for emerging shells in the water soaked sand. All afternoon we swam, ran races in the sand, threw the girls into the water and basically had a great time.

Finally, supper rolled around and Jorie, our Youth Director's wife, started cooking the hot dogs, hamburgers and whatever else people brought. The food didn't have to be gourmet, of course, for everything just tasted great with its charcoal flavor. Soon, the sun began to set, so we gathered up some long sticks along the grassy area and made s'mores. The melted chocolate and marshmallow on graham crackers really made our day!

Soon, our Youth Director, Al Baines, told everyone to gather around the fire so we could start our meeting. Our teen group was called Cheshire Teens, and it was an outreach group to the high school kids in three local townships in central Connecticut. Each week we'd meet either at the church or at some preplanned event, like a pool party, a bowling night, a miniature golf night, etc. Since I was the song leader, I passed out the Young Life books and got everyone singing at the top of their voices. Most of the beach goers had already left by now, so the group just sang out at the top of their voices. A little later we had a couple of skits, which my friend Steve and I had worked on all week, trying to be funny enough to get everyone laughing. Sometimes we were a success, but often we bumbled things up and got mocked out...but, even that was great fun!

After a half hour of this stuff, I gave the "podium" back to Al, who would normally bring a 15 minute outreach-type talk about Christ to the group. But, this week, he invited a guy by the name of Herb McCauley to speak. Herb was a big guy, well over six feet tall and looked like a lineman for the Dallas Cowboys. But, he was a gentle sort of guy when he speaking about the Savior he knew and loved, Jesus

Christ. I'll never forget that challenging message he presented to that group of fun-loving teenagers.

"The World Has Not Yet Seen One Totally Committed to God"

All of us listened intently, but that challenge didn't leave my mind for quite a while. Here we were, just a raggedy bunch of carefree young people enjoying life somewhat self-centeredly and without any inspiring thoughts about the future, God or about reality (other than fun in the sun and sand). But, Herb was trying to get us to think about more than just fooling around for a day at the beach. He wanted us to think beyond simple life pleasures and a cursory commitment to Christ. He wanted us to realize that God has so much more than all this stuff, if only we would open up our minds and hearts to what his Son had to say in the Bible. And, if we would dare to consider the possibility of doing that without reservation, we might experience something unbelievably fantastic in our spiritual lives, which too many believers just don't care enough to obtain.

Well, the meeting ended and all of us slowing inched our way back to our cars for the trip home. I don't know how many of my friends were as impacted by that simple yet profound talk, but the darkness of night couldn't drown out the light of truth that had crept into my foggy teen brain. It helped me immensely over the years to stay in close communication and commitment to my Lord and Savior.

So, how about you, friend? Are you at all excited about the possibilities of really experiencing great things from your relationship with Christ? You don't have to be a Pastor or a missionary to see God work into your life some fantastic blessings and opportunities for service. You just have to be wanting and willing enough to give God your best and to stay on track by faith.

I hope this book will help you with the fundamentals of Christian living, so that together we can experience all that God has for us. But, it's up to each one of us to reach out and apply these truths, for God isn't about to push his *best* upon someone who is satisfied with the *least* of his grace. How much do you want it, friend? It's waiting...and it's yours for the taking! Remember...

"The world STILL has not yet seen one totally committed to God"

Have you ever dreamed of being a published author?

If you are interested,
GET STARTED TODAY by visiting
FreeChrisitianPublishing.com

- 📖 *An exciting offer for authors who seek a do-it-yourself publishing experience. FOR FREE!*

- 📖 *Enjoy an ultimate level of control over your publishing journey with user-friendly online tools!*

- 📖 *Purchase books as you need them with our print on-demand, lightning-fast printing process!*

CPSIA information can be obtained
at www.ICGtesting.com
Printed in the USA
BVHW01s2308220218
508909BV00007B/71/P

9 781630 500283